"In a ministry culture often driven by urgency and efficiency, this book offers wisdom, clarity, and freedom."
Jonathan D. Holmes, Executive Director, CCEF

"If you're like me, trying to balance a number of responsibilities while wearing multiple hats, you will benefit from *Shepherding Time*. With brief chapters, helpful reflection questions, and clear action steps, this book will serve you well."
Juan R. Sanchez, Senior Pastor, High Pointe Baptist Church, Austin, TX; coauthor of *Reaching Your Child's Heart*

"*Shepherding Time* helps pastors examine their heart motives and relationship with God when stewarding both their callings and their time in light of ultimate and eternal purposes."
Mark Tatlock, President, The Master's Academy International

"Rush Witt and Joe Keller offer meaningful counsel to the church leader trying to be faithful both at home and in his local church. Their years of combined ministry experience show in a book that is accessible, honest, and full of practical action steps."
Ryan Robertson, President, Reaching & Teaching International

"Rush and Joe give busy shepherds a theological framework combined with genuinely helpful tools that I have not found anywhere else."
T. J. Freeman, Senior Pastor, Christ Church, Wellsboro, PA; executive director, The Brainerd Institute for Rural Ministry

"Pastors struggle with time management because everything matters and everyone needs them now. Witt and Keller finally wrote the book that addresses that real tension."
Chris Kouba, Lead Pastor, United City Church, Humble, TX; podcast host, *Step Up*

"*Shepherding Time* helps pastors think wisely about how to steward their limited hours for the sake of their people, families, and mission."
Scott Zeller, Executive Vice President of Churches, Acts 29

"If your time is overrun by the busyness of ministry and the tyranny of the urgent, Joe and Rush are very capable guides."
Deepak Reju, Senior Pastor, Ogletown Baptist Church, Newark, DE; author of *On Guard*

"Rush Witt and Joe Keller have set a wise course of action for pastors. By being proactive and thoughtful, pastors can redeem precious, God-given time."
Benjamin L. Gladd, Executive Director, The Carson Center for Theological Renewal

"Witt and Keller bring fresh biblical wisdom to productivity, helping pastors shepherd time without false guilt or neglect. This book helps pastors serve faithfully."

Dwayne Milioni, Lead Pastor; seminary professor; cofounder, the Pillar Network

"Keller and Witt provide practical, Christ-centered tools that have helped me become a wiser and more faithful steward of the time God has entrusted to me."

Timothy St. John, Counseling Pastor, Lighthouse Community Church, Torrance, CA; author of *After Church Hurt*

"You will be convicted, encouraged, and helped as you rethink how you use your time to maximize ministry effectiveness and do all for the glory of God."

Garrett Higbee, President, Soul Care Consulting International; director, Lead Healthy Retreats

"Witt and Keller give insight and care to categories of shepherding, time management, pastoral priorities, and rest. Take a personal retreat and prayerfully read this book."

Mike Seaver, Lead Pastor, Risen Hope Church, Summerville, SC; church plant coordinator, Sovereign Grace Churches

"This book is a rich source of both biblical wisdom and practical suggestions for how pastors can steward their time well. It will serve pastors to read and think about this essential topic so that they can use their time in ways that honor the Lord and serve the people of God."

Matthias Lohmann, Pastor, FEG Munich, Germany; chairman, Evangelium21; 9Marks speaker

"Rush and Joe have developed a thorough understanding of time management and our common struggles with it, and they deliver helpful strategy from pastors for pastors. Your ministry will be blessed by your timely engagement with this book!"

Adam Bailie, Senior Lead Pastor, Christ Church, Greensboro, NC

"I am grateful for these two gospel-shaped men who are passionate about using their time for the glory of God. Apply the message of this book to your every day as you seek to redeem your time with the one life you have to live."

Daniel S. Dumas, CEO, Red Buffalo

Shepherding Time

A Pastor's Guide to Time Management

Rush Witt and Joe Keller

New Growth Press
newgrowthpress.com

New Growth Press, Greensboro, NC 27401
Newgrowthpress.com

Cover Design: Faceout Books, faceoutstudio.com
Interior Typesetting/Ebook: Lisa Parnell, lparnellbookservices.com

ISBN: 978-1-64507-655-1 (paperback)
ISBN: 978-1-64507-656-8 (ebook)

Library of Congress Cataloging-in-Publication Data on file

Printed in Colombia

30 29 28 27 26 1 2 3 4 5

Contents

Foreword

I HAVE HAD the privilege of traveling across the world to visit local churches on each of the inhabited continents. I have been able to meet with pastors who minister in fast-paced global cities and in slow-paced rural villages. I have been able to spend time with pastors who are at the cutting edge of technology and those whose homes have yet to gain electricity or running water. I have learned from pastors in full-time ministry positions and pastors who rise long before the sun to tend to their cashew grove or rubber trees before they can begin to tend to their church. There are a few things that bind all of these faithful pastors together: their commitment to the Word of God, to prayer, and to shepherding the flock, and their shared struggle to manage their time well.

It is not only pastors who struggle with time management, of course. Yet pastors face particular challenges with their time that are not often addressed by the many books, guides, and programs. They have a unique collection of responsibilities and a unique structure of accountability. On any given day, they may be expected to exposit a text, counsel an addict, lead a premarital class, chair a meeting, and pray at the bed of a dying man. Because the work is never done, few pastors feel confident that they have used their time well. And perhaps of greater concern, few pastors feel confident that their parishioners believe they have used their time well either.

It is for these reasons that I'm thankful for this new book from Rush Witt and Joe Keller. They write as pastors to pastors—as shepherds to those who wish to shepherd their time confidently, successfully, and in a way that honors the Lord. They would be the first to admit that they have not mastered the art of time management, yet they have certainly made great strides in understanding how God means for them to use their time wisely and effectively. Their book is a powerful combination of biblical truths and practical pointers that draws from the deep wells of ancient wisdom and the frontlines of modern innovation. It avoids the heavy hand of the law to focus instead on grace. It guides pastors into a fresh understanding of how to use their time for the good of their church and the glory of God.

If you are already in pastoral ministry or training for it, I'm certain that *Shepherding Time* will prove to be a great gift to you. It will challenge, inform, and instruct you. Better yet, it will free you from false expectations—whether your own or other people's—so you can have confidence that you are honoring God with the time he has given you.

Tim Challies
Author of *Do More Better*, www.challies.com

Chapter 1
The Gift of Time

A FEW YEARS ago, HBO created a documentary about Berkshire Hathaway founder Warren Buffett titled *Becoming Warren Buffett*.[1] One scene on Buffett's view of time management caught viewers' attention in a special way. Speaking about his legendary protection of his time, Buffett made a fascinating offhand comment. He highlighted his notable timeliness and his insistence that people around him exercise a firm respect for time. He said, "I can buy anything I want, basically, but I can't buy time." Time is the one commodity he can't buy more of. It's a limited resource. It's finite. He has the same twenty-four hours in a day that the rest of us have.

An astounding revelation! Warren Buffett—a multibillionaire—sees time, not money, as his most valuable commodity. He knows no matter what endeavors he develops or how much money he amasses, he cannot buy or program into his life more time. Thus, he fears wasting it. Notice the key truth embedded in that story: How you think about time shapes your relationship to time. Every day, Buffett, perhaps unknowingly, borrows a principle precious to the Puritans.

The English preacher Thomas Watson wrote, "Time is a precious commodity, but how prodigally do many waste it! Time is the measure of our lives, and the loadstone of eternity; to trifle away time is to trifle away the soul."[2] What a powerful thought! Read that again.

In his work *Precious Remedies Against Satan's Devices*, Puritan Thomas Brooks wrote, "Time is a talent, and God will call you to account for how you have spent it. There is nothing more precious than time, and yet nothing of which we are more prodigal."[3]

While we may not share Buffett's financial world, we can admire his remarkable conscientiousness. He refuses to be enslaved to his schedule or the relentless demands of his work.

As pastors, we find Buffett's level of control both enviable and entirely foreign. In our combined ministry experience, we have spent years in the trenches of local church ministry, and we have often struggled to treat time with that same level of sober stewardship. In the life of a shepherd, the challenge rarely arises from a lack of work; instead, it comes from an abundance of good work. On any given Tuesday, we are faced with a dozen "best" ways to spend an hour: a sermon that needs depth, a grieving member who needs a visit, a leader who needs mentoring, or a family that needs a present husband and father.

We know the feeling of sitting at our desks, surrounded by these competing callings: a stack of books open for a series on the Psalms, a list of hospital visits to make, and a mounting pile of administrative tasks that feel essential to the health of the church. In that moment, we realize we aren't simply busy but reactive, trying to serve everyone well. Our schedules no longer serve as a tool for ministry; they become a master that we struggle to please.

In those moments, we remind each other that the *conflicting priorities* of ministry are not just items on a list; they are people with souls and responsibilities given to us by God. We find ourselves constantly torn between the needs of the sheep, the needs of our own homes, and the specific callings God has placed on our lives. We realize that without a clear, biblical framework for our days, we would continue to be driven by the loudest "ping" or the most recent crisis.

We are writing this book out of our collective experiences with shepherding time. We have felt overwhelmed by the sheer volume of good tasks and deeply unsure of how to make the best use of the time we have been given. We haven't mastered our minutes, but we know the importance of finding a way to honor the Lord with them. This is our attempt to move away from the frantic pace of chaotic calendaring, and toward a grace-centered, intentional stewardship of the days God has numbered for us.

The Pastoral Tension

While Buffett fears wasting a finite commodity, we often find ourselves fearing a different kind of failure: neglecting a soul. Buffett sees time as a resource to be managed; as pastors, we see it as a context for worship. And that makes the pressure feel much heavier.

In our combined fifty years of pastoral ministry, we have not sat on the sidelines. We have planted churches, shepherded congregations through crises, and counseled families in their darkest hours. Yet, despite those years of experience, we have spent much of our ministry in the "too-muchness" of the calling. We know the specific, heavy exhaustion of a schedule that never seems to honor the God we serve or the people we love.

Picture the common rhythm of a Tuesday morning. You are in your study, finally finding your stride in the text for Sunday's sermon. Your heart is engaged with the Word, and the "ministry of the Word" feels like the priority it should be. Then, the phone rings. A deacon's father has just passed away.

In an instant, your focus must pivot. As you grab your keys to head to the hospital, your mind begins to race. You realize you still have three unreturned emails about the upcoming budget deadline. You remember you promised your spouse you'd be home for dinner to help with the kids. By the time you reach the hospital parking lot, you aren't just thinking about the grieving family; you are calculating the "cost" of the visit against the rest of your life.

You know the feeling. It's the whiplash of moving from a budget meeting to a hospital bedside, then back to a staff lunch, all while trying to maintain the spiritual posture of a shepherd. It's the nagging "time guilt" that follows you home—the sense that by being faithful to the church, you are being unfaithful to your family, or by resting, you are failing your flock.

We didn't write this book because we have perfectly mastered every fifteen-minute block on our calendars. We wrote it because we reached a point where we were overwhelmed. We were tired of feeling like we were constantly behind, perpetually distracted, and unsure of how to make the best use of our time in a calling that is never truly "finished."

This book is the result of our own search for a better way. We wanted to move past the frantic pursuit of secular efficiency and find a biblical theology of stewardship—one that offers pastors confidence and grace instead of just a longer to-do list. We wrote this because we needed a way to shepherd our time so that we could more faithfully shepherd our people. Do you think of time as your precious commodity, a divinely entrusted talent? Every person, whether they are a pastor or parishioner, has access to the same 168 hours per week. No more, no less. But not all people (and certainly not all pastors) will use those hours to the same effect. You don't need to understand Einstein's theory of relativity to know this important fact: The limited nature of your time means you have choices to make. While the amount of time cannot be altered, its use can and must be shepherded. Thus, every wise pastor affirms the prayer of Moses, "Teach us to number our days carefully so that we may develop wisdom in our hearts" (Psalm 90:12). God bestows his good gift of time on everyone. Though he ordains some to have a longer breadth of life, he has determined each of us will have the same units of time. Sixty seconds in a minute. Sixty minutes in an hour. Twenty-four hours in a day. One hundred sixty-eight hours in a week. As a result, we must set our minds not on how we can get more time, but rather how will we make the God-glorifying most of it (Proverbs 16:9; Matthew 6:27).

One of the great mysteries of the world centers on the distinction between the Creator and his creatures. He stands above time. God transcends the natural world with omnipresence and omniscience. He does not need time to exist or function in any way. Yet God created time for his creatures: to structure our world, to mark our lives, and to give us a context in which we would glorify and enjoy him (Acts 17:24–28). In this way, time serves not as a mere commodity but as the context in which every moment of God's redemptive plan unfolds. Stop and ponder that for a moment longer.

What a thought! God created time for the people of his world to live out his created design. God placed his unfolding plan of redemption in the context of time. Therefore, time serves as the very atmosphere in which we live out every moment he ordained for our ultimate good and his ultimate glory (Psalm 139:16).

And yet we must confess we've spent vast amounts of this most precious commodity on frivolous matters. What a waste of a good gift! Yet hope remains! The God of time intends to help us redeem our time.

The answer to this problem amounts to a change of heart and mind about the gift of time. Pastors need a renewed vision of its purpose and potential in their lives and in the lives of others who serve God's people. May this book help you shepherd time wisely in the present moment and with eternity in view.

Maximizing the Impact of Time

A pastor's calendar may look like one long list of events, but the impact of those hours differs dramatically. Therefore, every faithful shepherd must strategize the use of his time for the most effective impact. In fact, pastoral wisdom comes through the shepherd's ability to discern the impact of each moment and then apply himself accordingly.

Think about some examples where impact differs between tasks. On any given day, you must navigate between things like sitting in a hospital waiting room and attending the youth group play. Pastors must think through the options of engaging in bus-stop conversation with an unbeliever and the post–Bible study conversation with a discouraged church member. You must balance your time between investing in leaders and consulting with a staff member. All these tasks carry a weight of impact, and each has a rightful place in the pastor's work. Yet to make the strongest overall impact, we must order our pastoral world. To drive home this important truth, we want to tell you a story.

Killers, fillers, and instillers

Our story finds three pastors living in three towns. The first pastor was a *time killer*. He always looked "busy," and yet much of his week slipped away into distractions and half-finished tasks. He lingered lazily over endless emails, scrolled through newsfeeds, and padded his schedule with tasks requiring little energy. He killed time, and with it, the opportunities God placed before him. The flock felt his presence little.

The second was a *time filler*. He kept active, was never idle. His days remained stacked with meetings, visits, committees, errands, and events. But his heart was thin. He filled his time with tasks, but much of it proved motion without ministry. The congregation saw him, and yet the quality of his efforts amounted to little in the end.

The third was a *time instiller*. He planned his ministry and administered his plan. Every aspect of his leadership carried weight and possibility. He sat in the hospital waiting room not only to pass the hours but to instill comfort and pray as an embodiment of God's presence. He attended the students' early morning Bible study not merely to fill space on the schedule but to instill the Word into young hearts. He brought into meetings, living rooms, coffee shops, and even sideline conversations an intentionality to instill the marrow of ministry into the people entrusted to him.

Invest with purpose

One killed time, one filled time, but the time shepherd instilled time, and God's people flourished. The goal of the instiller is to ensure that no moment is merely spent, but that every hour is invested with eternal purpose. However, this high calling of instilling value requires a sense of holy urgency, for the opportunity to shepherd our people is as fleeting as it is precious.

So the question is not *whether* your hours will be spent—they will be—but whether, when the Master returns, they will have been spent on what was merely urgent or on what was eternally important.

Time Waits for No One

In *The Canterbury Tales* we read these ironically timeless words: "Time and tide wait for no man."[4] The Clerk's Tale presents the scene of a peasant named Griselda, who marries a marquis and must prove her loyalty. The Clerk, who tells the tale, draws out this pithy line to show that not even a noble ruler can stop the relentless turning of time. Indeed, the tide of life and death rises and falls with no one to stop it.

Pastoral life brings so many incredible blessings to our lives. For many, on any given day, it seems our biggest problem is choosing between the litany of possible good works laid out before us. God has so filled our lives with good things that we must wrangle with choosing between them. You shouldn't hear this as bragging. Your pastoral life faces the very same reality. Yes, you have hardships and struggles like us all. But think about it: The pastoral life never lacks for rewarding ministry to accomplish. And it makes our shepherding of time even more foundational.

We feel the pressures of pastoral time, in part, because of the relentless nature of time. Time does not pause, rewind, or grant do-overs. We've heard it said, "Four things do not come back: the spoken word, the sped arrow, the past life, and the neglected opportunity."[5] While all four deserve our attention, the last one holds special significance to us as pastors. Ministry always takes place in the moving stream of time. Pastor Thomas Adams wrote, "Every hour hath wings, and there is no moment passing from us but it flies up to the Maker of time, and bears him true tidings how we have used it."[6] Picture the hourglass which John Piper flips over, shouting "for the kingdom and the family!"—every grain of sand falls whether we use it well or not.

Every minute counts (Ecclesiastes 3:1). If you embrace this reality with us, we will see together the way it changes our approach to everything. A pastor's calendar serves not simply as a record of tasks and appointments but as an account of stewardship before the Lord, our Chief Shepherd.

Therefore, today is the day because time and tide wait for no pastor. Procrastination hovers as a great enemy of shepherding time, and we must kill it. And yet we are convinced that in this life our battles with time stewardship will see no end. Walter Henegar recalled his own difficulty making the most of time, saying, "All of a sudden I could see myself clearly. There I was, buzzing diligently around the room, while that thing, the one thing I needed to do most, sat unheeded in the middle of it. I wasn't just a procrastinator; I was a work-around-er."[7] Today is the day to visit, to call, to counsel, to pray.

> A pastor's calendar serves as an account of stewardship before the Lord.
>
> ~ ~ ~
>
> *How does remembering that time belongs to Christ reshape the way you plan your week?*

Time will wait for no pastor. But by grace, biblical wisdom helps us redeem wasted time (Ephesians 5:16). Don't merely watch the sands slip through the glass. Together we can learn to shepherd the moments, steward the hours, and offer each season of ministry as a good gift back to the Lord. Today is the day to shepherd time.

Time Is Central to Effective Ministry

As pastors we must think deeply about many things. This book will help you think wisely about time, what it means, and how it works in your pastoral context. This book does not merely aim to make you efficient with your time. *Shepherding Time* offers more than a formula for success, a time-tracking gimmick, or a plan to get more out of your remaining days. The shelves are full of books and resources designed to help you monitor your moments or get more done. This book will help you bring time into clearer view, as a central part of your pastoral life and ministry.

Pastors know the value of seeing all aspects of life through a shepherd's eyes, and that includes the subject of time. And you know the pastor's schedule contains unique challenges due to the unpredictable nature and variety of needs that arise. Thus, the average pastor needs a unique kind of help in this area. Time is a priceless commodity for any spiritual leader.

Two big truths will govern the remaining pages: First, God has limited your time, and second, he wants you to use your time for good. Unpacking these truths at the outset will lay out the two important tracks on which we can run forward together.

Time Is Limited

Every week offers you 168 hours. Time is one thing you cannot gain more of. Are your eyes bad? The surgeon can give you new ones. Do you need more money? Apply for a better job. Want more time? No answer. Everyone faces the same reality. Ask not how you can get more time but how you can use it more wisely.

Paul gives a robust exhortation about the wisdom of time-attentiveness. "Pay careful attention, then, to how you walk—not as unwise people but as wise—making the most of the time, because the days are evil. So don't be foolish, but understand what the Lord's will is" (Ephesians 5:15–17). Perhaps the most striking words in the passage point to the evilness of our days. Why should you give attention to your time? The days are evil. The fallen world order works against the proper use of time for God's glory. If left unattended, the curse of sin will eat away at the fabric of our time, leaving holes of lost opportunities.

Feel the profound significance of this reality and the preciousness of time by recalling that this present hour, minute, or second will never exist again. Look at *today* on your calendar and know there will never be another today. Just as the ancients told of Cronus devouring his children, so too does time, relentless and impartial, consume the days we fail to redeem. Truly, today is a "vapor that appears for a little while, then vanishes" (James 4:14). You know it's true when you stop at your desk to check email for a moment and suddenly realize you lost half of an afternoon. Among Jonathan Edwards's Seventy Resolutions sits, "5. Resolved, never to lose one moment of time; but improve it the most profitable way I possibly can."[8] The limitation of time means that though we may sometimes be labeled as a know-it-all, none of us will ever become do-it-alls. We live as finite creatures in every respect. This realization forces prayerful discernment about what matters most.

You might imagine our common need for discernment around the topics of time and productivity. Think of a jar, and next to it a pile of big rocks, a pile of pebbles, and a pile of sand. You need to put all three piles in the jar. You quickly realize the only way to accomplish it. You must move the big rocks first, then the pebbles, then the sand. In a similar way, the precious time you have will neatly fit into your life if you exercise discernment about the place and order of your affairs.

Some attribute to John Wesley (though of uncertain origin) the famous quip, "Do all the good you can, by all the means you can, in all the ways you can, in all the places you can, at all the times you can, to all the people you can, as long as ever you can." Though it displays disordered priorities, this encouragement still serves us well. In the spirit of it, we ask you to continue reflecting on your life and time as the book moves forward. Since your days are numbered by God, how many of them are already behind you? How have your days been used? What will you do with the remaining ones?

Time Is for Doing Good

As we embark on a journey into the unpredictable realm of pastoral time, we need to keep another key truth in mind: God has designed time with a purpose. Although we do want to think of time as a commodity, remember it exists not merely as a commodity for us to leverage. But time provides a purposeful context for good. Time is not neutral; it always functions with a sense of purpose. That's why there remains a time for everything under the sun (Ecclesiastes 3:1).

Thus, we do not shepherd time to do more things or merely work with greater efficiency. Shepherding time allows us to embrace the vast and endless goodness of God's calling on our lives. Shepherding time enables us to engage in effective gospel ministry, promote kingdom flourishing, and flourish in our own gifts.

In Scripture, the goal of time is to do good. The flourishing of the Christian life stands out as the very best good we can do. Consider the various analogies which Scripture uses to describe the nature of spiritual leadership. Find the central thread running through each of them: *flourishing*.

John and Peter describe ministry in terms of a shepherd and flock (John 10:11–16; 1 Peter 5:2–3). Pastors serve as shepherds who lead, feed, and protect. As a result, the flock flourishes, not because the shepherd stays busy at tasks, but because he invests time and energy in what really matters. As he watches carefully, guides patiently, and leads the sheep through green pastures, the sheep flourish.

Paul and James reflect the pastor's role to that of a farmer in a field (1 Corinthians 3:6–9; 2 Timothy 2:6; James 5:7). The kingdom grows like a flourishing field under the pastor-farmer's labor. He plants with wisdom, waters generously, and waits prayerfully for God to give the glorious increase. Thus, the pastor in God's field cannot rush the harvest's development, but he certainly can hinder it through undisciplined neglect. In this way, kingdom flourishing depends not on a pastor's frantic busyness but on his steady and faithful investment. The field flourishes.

Paul also offers the temple builder analogy, in which pastors serve as builders who lay strong foundations and build up the church (1 Corinthians 3:10–15; Ephesians 2:19–22). With Christ as cornerstone, he pictures local churches as temples which grow and develop into a dwelling place for his Spirit. Wise builders don't merely slap a bunch of stones together. Instead, they steward time to design, measure, and carefully build strength toward the ultimate vision. The building flourishes.

Take these analogies and more, and we see again the role of pastors who shepherd. They equip the saints for the work of ministry, promoting and mobilizing others to follow Christ (Ephesians 4:11–12). They do this most faithfully when they minister with a keen sense of time.

God has created and called every Christian as his workmanship, and every ministry leader has the unmatched privilege of promoting this ultimate good in a world full of profound need. Let's move from here to think a bit more about God's design for time to produce redemptive good in the world.

In Colossians 4:5, Paul directly ties wise stewardship of time to doing good before a watching world. We carry into the rest of this book the reminder that our time never functions in neutrality but always with a missional punch. Every moment of time presents an opportunity to show Christ's goodness. Paul makes a further point you might not think of as time-focused. In 1 Thessalonians 5:15, he writes, "See to it that no one repays evil for evil to anyone, but always pursue what is good for one another and for all." Many people find it easy to pass right over a verse like this, thinking about it as a general call to do good. But look more closely at that word "pursue." Paul uses a Greek word, translated *pursue*, which combines both urgency and effort over time. Every pursuit in life requires a strong sense of time because without it the pursuit falls flat. Look at the *pursuits* of your life. Each and every one requires a solid investment of your time. To the degree that you steward your time, you will also achieve your pursuit.

> God has created and called every Christian as his workmanship.
>
> ~ ~ ~
>
> *How does this relate to the pastoral calling to shepherd time?*

Finally, read again Paul's words to the Ephesians: "For we are his workmanship, created in Christ Jesus for good works, which God prepared ahead of time for us to do" (Ephesians 2:10). Did you catch that? God prepared our good works ahead of the time in which they would be done. Truly, God's intentions for our time—past, present, future—rest securely in his hands (Psalm 31:15). What more motivation do we need to take our time seriously as leaders of God's people?

Time Is for Shepherding

At this point, we need to arrive at a firm conclusion from the basics of time we just considered. God has given to us the good gift of time, a limited resource by which he intends to use us to accomplish an unlimited good. Read that critical sentence again. Moving from biblical foundations to pastoral implications, what conclusion can we draw? Every one of us needs to steward our time with intentionality, humility, and hope. The point does not call us merely to find something good to do (as we often tell our children), but we must answer the question, "What specific good should I do today, or this hour, or in this moment?" Answering the question requires a keen sense of stewardship, priority, and vision. The needed effort does not happen by accident. Just as God created time with divine intention, he calls us to intentional effort and leadership in stewarding this limited resource to the best effect.

As we move forward, a surprising reality awaits. Stewarding time as pastors is not a mere exercise in practicality. Instead, we find pastoral time management flows from a consideration of the art of shepherding time.

Reflection Questions

1. How do you think focusing on Christ rather than our failures can help us better use our time?
2. How does image-bearing relate to time?
3. God has created and called every Christian as his workmanship. How does this relate to the pastoral calling to shepherd time?
4. As pastors, we see time as a context for worship. How does shepherding time increase worship in the heart of the pastor?

Action Step

Begin each day with a dedicated time of reflection using Psalm 90:12. Write out what you perceive as your most valuable uses of time each day. List three activities you can embrace that day to treat your time as a precious commodity.

Chapter 2
The Art of Shepherding Time

WE GREW UP on a heavy diet of movies and television. As we wrangle with the challenge of pastoral time management, we're drawn back to our childhood and the haunting intro to Rod Serling's classic, *The Twilight Zone*. "You're traveling through another dimension, a dimension not only of sight and sound but of mind. A journey into a wondrous land whose boundaries are that of imagination. That's the signpost up ahead—your next stop, *The Twilight Zone*!"[1]

We've spent significant hours wrestling through time-related issues in our own lives and ministries, and we know the difficulties of pastoral time management. Sometimes it resembles a disorienting trip through the twilight zone. We're eager to share key insights from Scripture and experience with you, our fellow time shepherds.

In this book, we are your guides through another dimension. This is a journey to examine the unique aspects of pastoral time and how we can grow to faithfully steward it. That's why the book you're holding is so important. If you're like us (and we're wagering you are), you're a good pastor who wants to serve well in your calling, but every now and again you run into troubles with time that make you question whether you're going at it the best way. You're not alone.

As a minister of the gospel, you consider all of life as a context for making and multiplying disciples. From casual conversations to public proclamations and everything in between, faithful pastors see every area and detail of life as an opportunity for gospel ministry.

> As a minister of the gospel, you consider all of life as a context for making and multiplying disciples.
>
> ~ ~ ~
>
> *What does that look like in your ministry?*

Time works the same way. We must learn to use our time as a context for ministry. This shifts our mindset from focusing on efficiencies to focusing on effectiveness. Certainly, there are important ways that shepherds should manage their time efficiently. Many books on this topic could help you. However, the deeper aspiration of *Shepherding Time* is not merely to spend time, but to consider how time can be best used for love and good deeds.

In our pursuit of love and good deeds, every person perceives time differently. Parents see time through the lens of child training. Police officers focus on the time when enforcing laws. Teachers think of time in the classroom. Shepherds see time as a context for worship in all areas of life and try to help others do the same.

Pastoral Time Morphs

Pastors have a unique challenge to manage different kinds of time in any given week. Time for solitude. Time for preparation. Time for counsel. Time for grieving. There is also time that is related to our roles. Time with family. Time with friends. Time with church members. Time spent with community folks. For the pastor, as much as anyone, "There is an occasion for everything, and a time for every activity under heaven" (Ecclesiastes 3:1).

Thus, a pastor's time is not stagnant; it morphs from one kind of time to another. It is not uncommon for a pastor to be in the same place but experience different kinds of time. He learns quickly that a routine phone call from a senior saint can morph family time into care and crisis time. This reality poses the significant challenge of unpredictability. It takes a unique mindfulness and situational awareness to recognize what kind of time dimension you are in, and then to help others know what kind of time you are living out before them (Ephesians 5:15–16).

Time dimensions often morph when a pastor least expects it. For instance, I may think I'm living in a dimension of time for friendship while those around me think we're in a dimension of time dedicated to pastoral care. Golf provides a good illustration. Imagine that you're out with three guys from church for an early morning tee time. Your foursome plays through the first nine holes with lighthearted joy and friendly banter. A significant counseling session emerges at Hole 10. You feel time swirling from golf time into counseling time, as one of the guys asks you what he should do about the serious rift in his marriage. In the middle of your back swing, leisure time has morphed into counsel time. These unsettling shifts happen to every person, irrespective of life stage or vocation. But with the responsibility of pastoring in every moment, time morphing experiences bring a sobering reality to pastors. It brings the startling reminder that we carry a heightened challenge, as pastors, to shepherd our time.

Have you experienced the startling shifts of time in your own life and ministry? We once asked for advice about this from a seasoned pastor. "Yeah, of course," he said. "You just have to learn to go with the flow." At the time that sounded well and good, but I found the answer too simple. There's more to the issue than simply learning to relax and pivot or just go with the flow. It requires a keen ability to see and foresee the ever-shifting dimensions of our time. Richard Baxter warns in *The Reformed Pastor*, "Be careful in the spending of your time: it is so short, and so precious, that it must be carefully redeemed."[2]

> It takes a unique mindfulness and situational awareness to recognize what kind of time dimension you are in.
>
> ~ ~ ~
>
> *How can you recognize when you are not considering this?*

The unpredictability of pastoral circumstances creates significant occasions for pastoral frustration, perhaps even resentment of pastoral life. I've felt it myself and seen it in others. The fact that time can shift with such unpredictability provokes a feeling of instability. For some pastors, resentment grows with the feeling that "I can't enjoy a round of golf because some unexpected conversation or distraction could pop out of the bushes without fair warning."

We have good news. Unpredictability remains a reality, but it need not deter us from enjoying our calling or the many blessings of pastoral life. We can meet the nuanced rhythms of ministry with joy. Our days may feel, at times, chaotic—as if there is no reliable direction or plan—but when your heart as a pastor is to model, apply, and encourage worship in all circumstances, time morphs can be shepherded. Learning to move gracefully from one conversation or circumstance to another is not only possible but also an invaluable skill. To develop this skill, we must first recognize the distinct landscapes where our ministry unfolds. In the following sections, we will explore how to navigate these diverse contexts of pastoral time, distinguishing between the structured rhythms of the church gathered and the fluid, often surprising needs of the church scattered.

Navigating the Contexts of Pastoral Time

As if it wasn't difficult enough to navigate the unpredictable shifts of pastoral time, the various contexts of pastoral time further complicate things. Spiritual leadership often requires an intentionality to discern the need of the moment. By capturing a sense of the contexts of ministry, we can increase our grasp on this unique challenge of pastoral time. We can frame out pastoral time into two big categories, then we can drill down into the nuances of each one. We can mark the foundational division between ministry contexts by drawing a line between *the church gathered* and *the church scattered.*

Faithful voices of the past have clarified this division of the church's life into two main states: gathered under her elders and scattered on mission. Trusted pastor, Tim Keller, develops this distinction. He taught us the church is not just a collection of individuals saved from the world but a new society sent into the world. God's people gather as churches to be shaped by the Word and the sacraments, and then we scatter to be salt and light in every area of life.[3]

These two states provide the foundational starting point by which we can think about shepherding time. Now we can drill down into each state—*gathered* and *scattered.*

The Church Gathered

All faithful pastors agree about the importance of holding Sunday as the most important day of the week. On Sundays, we have the privilege of serving the people of God as we mobilize around the preaching of God's Word, the fellowship of our faith, and the pastoral care we've been called to provide. None of this can happen without careful preparation. And careful preparation cannot happen without a careful stewardship of time.

Pastors on Sunday are like runners on marathon race day. Two runners have wildly different experiences. One runner follows a customized marathon prep plan. In four-week training blocks, the plan assigns a variety of road running workouts designed to progressively strengthen their aerobic engine, foot speed, and running form. When the marathon date rolls around, the first runner meets the challenge with relative ease. By following the plan, running the marathon feels like the easy part. The hardest part—the training—is over, and the marathon is a joy.

Another runner's road-race adventure turns out exponentially worse. His lack of focused training produces a far different outcome. He lacks dietary discipline, starts training the week before the race, and doesn't watch even one YouTube video about how to complete a marathon in your forties. This poor runner walks the last two miles of the marathon slower than the race organizers who pass him as they clean up the cones and signage.

In a similar way, how a pastor shepherds time during the week will impact the joy and effectiveness of the Sunday gathering when the church comes together. This rhythm comprises a large part of our calling to shepherd our time. Pastoral time management matters not only because it helps us get things done, but also because it paves the way for the most important day of the week: Sunday. How we shepherd time Monday through Friday will set the course for how we shepherd souls on Sunday.

In fact, the ministry workweek is designed for that central purpose, that we might fully engage with God and his people on Sunday. Certainly, we do not intend to suggest one-on-one visitation ministry or personal study is less valuable; rather, Sunday holds a critical ministry of the week, and we do well to focus our time toward that end. But what exactly should our preparation focus on? Let's consider three areas of preparation.

Prepare to shepherd with presence

Pastors shepherd with presence in many ways. Remaining spiritually attuned, relationally engaged, and missionally intentional requires several things. First, pastors need to prayerfully prepare for Sunday. How easy it can be to go through the usual motions of weekly ministry without depending on the Lord! Prayer needs constant attention. Second, they need to engage authentically with those in front of them. In the midst of many moving parts, faithful pastors hone their focus on the lives and needs of the people in their congregations. And third, they need to keep the vision and mission in clear view. Mission drift happens when good but less important things pull us away from our central focus.

Prepare to feed with substance

Scripture and our own experience agree that feeding the congregation on the bread of Christ and his Word stands out as a pastor's primary task when the church gathers. This belief echoes the words of Calvin who said, "The preaching of the Word is the chief and most effective part of the ministry of the church."[4] Charles Spurgeon agrees: "I believe that the great ordinance of God, the pillar and ground of the truth in the Church of God, is the preaching of the Word."[5] When a pastor invests weekday hours in study, prayer, and reflection, he brings more than surface thoughts on Sunday—he provides deep, biblically-rooted nourishment for the souls and lives of God's people.

Prepare to shepherd with sensitivity

A true shepherd aims to care for the sheep among him, not only to move them in and out of position according to the morning schedule.

To make the most of our opportunities to personally care for souls on Sunday, we must exercise pastoral discipline during the week. Sunday morning worship is a Saturday night decision. For ministry leaders, Sunday morning is a Monday, Tuesday, Wednesday, Thursday, Friday, and Saturday decision. Truly, focused attention during the week remains the hands-down key which opens the door to profound spiritual care on Sunday.

While we labor through the week in preparation for the gathered ministry of the church, our stewardship must also extend to the unscripted hours after the benediction is spoken. This leads us to consider the unique challenges of caring for a flock that no longer sits in one room, but scatters throughout the local community, in homes, schools, and workplaces.

The Church Scattered

Pastoral ministry contains another special challenge when the church scatters into the world, between the key gatherings of the church on Sunday or Wednesday or other times. As mentioned above, when the members and pastors gather for worship and other discipleship opportunities, time runs along a fairly simple track. A program of activities, complete with start and end times, govern the gatherings. But when the flock scatters back to the places where they work, play, and live, the pastors return to their daily lives and schedules, as well.

Everyone knows church leaders only work on Sundays. What an incredible gig! One day on, six days off. Of course, nothing could be further from the truth, and the truth highlights one of the immense challenges of pastoral time management. Among the scattered church, the simple track of Sunday programming splinters into an entire network of ministry rails on which pastors must run. There is an almost endless list of responsibilities and tasks which await pastors during the week. It might be helpful to give a categorical list of the many good things awaiting every church leader Monday through Saturday:

Worship and preaching

- Weekly sermon preparation and delivery
- Leading worship services
- Planning special services (Christmas, Easter, baptisms, ordinations)
- Coordinating with worship/music leaders

Teaching and discipleship

- Adult Bible studies (weekday or weekend)
- Student/college Bible studies (often early morning or late night)
- One-on-one discipleship over meals or coffee
- Small group leadership or oversight
- Teaching at retreats, conferences, or seminars

Shepherding and care

- Counseling sessions (marriage, family, addiction, grief)
- Hospital visits and home visits
- Crisis intervention (emergencies, tragedies, unexpected events)
- Funerals and memorial services

- Weddings and premarital counseling
- Ongoing pastoral check-ins with members

Leadership and administration

- Elder meetings
- Deacon meetings
- Committee/team meetings (finance, missions, facilities, etc.)
- Staff planning and coordination
- Volunteer training and oversight
- Church-wide communication and planning

Community and outreach

- Attending community events (sporting events, school functions, civic gatherings)
- Meeting local leaders (school officials, city leaders)
- Evangelism and outreach efforts
- Local missions partnerships
- Benevolence and mercy ministries

Personal and denominational responsibilities

- Denominational gatherings or association meetings
- Continuing education (seminars, conferences, reading)
- Mentoring younger pastors or ministry leaders
- Writing (articles, devotionals, books)
- Personal spiritual disciplines (prayer, study, meditation)
- Personal physical health (diet, exercise, recuperation)
- Sabbath rest (reflection, recreation, interpersonal renewal)

These categories represent more than just a to-do list; they are the diverse "ministry rails" that compete for your attention every single day. Balancing these varied callings requires more than just high energy—it demands a deliberate strategy to ensure that nothing vital is left behind.

We all can feel overwhelmed when thinking about the six important days which stand between Sundays. Or you may feel trepidation because you struggle to formulate a workable plan to handle it all. You have 168 hours every week to serve the Lord and his church. Subtract for sleep, and you have 120 waking hours left between Monday morning and Saturday night. That equates to three full-time jobs. Brothers, you do not lack for time. More often, we lack a wise plan to put those hours to their greatest impact. But not for long!

Reflection Questions

1. As a minister of the gospel, you consider all of life as a context for making and multiplying disciples. What does that look like in your ministry?
2. It takes a unique mindfulness and situational awareness to recognize what kind of time dimension you are in. How can you recognize when you are not considering this?
3. Where is one area in which you can shepherd your time more intentionally?
4. Who might you invite into your world to hold you accountable or help you increase awareness?
5. Do you need to confess and repent for ways you have neglected or misused your time? Don't delay—redeem it.

Action Step

Outline the purpose of your pastoral role and how you believe time management aligns with fulfilling God's mission. Reflect on how you can adjust your schedule to better align with these purposes. What changes would you make today, given no restraints?

Chapter 3
Honoring Time Expectations

CHARLES AND ROGER pastor vastly different churches. Roger's church has thousands of people, while Charles's church has barely one hundred. Roger's church is much older and more established, while Charles's church was planted just a few years ago. Roger's church meets in the beautiful hills of California, while Charles's church meets in an urban enclave of a Midwestern city. Among many differences, one can point to a disappointing reality. People have left both churches over the years. Add them all together, and these churches could've multiplied into an untold number of churches.

Some people have left Roger's and Charles's churches for good reasons. They took a job promotion in another city. They had children and wanted to move back home near their grandparents. They left for the mission field or to plant a church. Others have left for less desirable reasons. Roger and Charles ask themselves why, and one answer rises to the top of the list: unmet expectations. Some expectations are simply unrealistic, and they go unmet for obvious reasons. And still other expectations are good and right, but our churches—leaders and members alike—did not step up to meet them.

Either way, a reason so many people struggle to join, stay, and grow in a church comes down to expectations. Thus, we will do ourselves a big service by learning to think carefully about the vast collection of expectations, especially those centered on how pastors and other church leaders use their time.

Pastoral Time Expectations

Gaining a firm and useful grasp on our time requires attention to the expectations in our lives. We all tend to think, *I don't worry about what other people think; I just live my life and everyone else can deal with it*. That kind of thinking might work for most people in the world, but pastors don't have the luxury of such an oblivious lifestyle (and no one should actually live this way). Pastors are, in fact, men of the people and should therefore care about the expectations of others. We should be careful to not cross over into the ever-alluring fear of man, in which we live for the opinions of others (Proverbs 29:25). And yet we must not throw pastoral caution to the wind and adopt the *I'm my own man* mentality.

The sheep under our care have expectations. How could they not? They have entrusted their souls (to one degree or another) to our oversight, and it comes with expectations. Church members expect us to be places and do things, and all of this requires time. Therefore, a significant part of shepherding our time well requires a healthy relationship with the expectations others bring to the various contexts of pastoral ministry.

Just as every city operates in a unique way, and every neighborhood in those cities has distinctive rhythms, so also every church holds certain expectations. Like the hub of a wheel, the role of the pastor and his use of pastoral time (sometimes even the use of his personal time) stands at the center. Think about your own church experience. Nearly all expectations intersect with how the pastor exercises his calling over time.

- One church member expects pastors to hold strict office hours, while another expects them to exercise public presence in the surrounding community.
- One member expects pastors to spend extended hours in sermon preparation, while another expects pastors to be always available for counseling and visitation.
- One member expects pastors to prioritize hospital visits and home visits, while another expects them to prioritize administrative leadership and strategic planning.
- One member expects pastors to devote much of their time to community outreach and evangelism, while another expects them to spend that same time discipling existing members.
- One member expects pastors to be in the church office during the day, while another expects them to be available in the evenings when working people are free.
- One member expects pastors to be heavily involved in youth activities, while another expects them to give primary attention to adult ministry and teaching.
- One member expects pastors to spend time building the online presence of the church (podcasts, social media, etc.), while another expects them to avoid online activities altogether, to maximize time for in-person shepherding.
- One member expects pastors to develop the church's denomination or network, while another sees pastors as only serving the local congregation.

Anyone can see the challenging work of shepherding time, and that it will almost always involve a failure to meet or understand some expectations. Keeping an attitude of humility and repentance helps us walk this delicate pathway through expectations, even in the face of failure. Most of the time, you cannot recognize expectations until you fall short of meeting one.

Effective pastors learn to create proper expectations, not eliminate them (1 Thessalonians 4:1). Expectations in the life of a pastor cannot be ignored or unaddressed. They need to be identified and engaged with the same pastoral care and concern as every other area of ministry.

You will find invaluable insights by identifying the major influences in your pastoral life and taking inventory of the expectations that shape them. You might consider meeting with a few key leaders or long-time members to gain their insights. How do they view pastoral time in general, and more specifically in relation to your ministry? What do they think are the major categories in which the pastor's time should be invested? Doing this does not mean you need to incorporate each expectation you hear, but you do need to get a clear sense of the expectations around you.

If you recently joined a church staff, the importance of this step cannot be overstated. And if you're a veteran leader of your current church, keeping tabs on expectations still holds immense value. Why do unmet expectations impact you so deeply? How does fear of failure or fear of man shape your response? What does it mean to engage unreasonable expectations with grace, without giving in at the wrong moments? Pastors cannot avoid these questions. In addition to shepherding time, we must proactively shepherd expectations—with ourselves, our families, and our congregations.

This is why shaping expectations is a ministry in itself. It sets the culture for how a church views time, ministry effort, and pastoral stewardship. And pastors do not have to navigate this alone. Invite others into this struggle by giving them permission to encourage and admonish you when they see misplaced expectations or destructive patterns of time guilt.

Biblical Time Expectations

On the topic of shepherding time, we will offer you many helpful tools, strategies, insights, cautions, and reminders. But none of them will make any real difference in your life and ministry if we fail to lay the necessary foundation.

Most pastors might bring to a book like this an attitude that says, "Just cut to the chase and tell me how to use my time better." And, yes, we also are chomping at the bit to get there. But first, we need to bring front and center the divine expectations revealed in Scripture. Even the most faithful pastors among us need the regular reminder of what Scripture expects of our calling, especially as it relates to how we fulfill that calling over time.

In an effort to keep the main thing the main thing, pastors should calibrate their hearts around seven categories of biblical expectations for pastors.

1. Prayer and the ministry of the Word

In Acts 6, the disciples form the office of deacon so that the pastors could focus on two interconnected ministries: prayer and the ministry of the Word (Acts 6:4). We conclude, then, pastors should intentionally assign a strong portion of time to praying and giving godly counsel and wisdom. D. A. Carson reminds us, "Much praying is not done because we do not plan to pray. We will not grow in prayer unless we plan to pray."[1]

The author of Acts uses the Greek word *proseuchē* (prayer).[2] In the context of pastoral leadership, the term implies a kind of work. Most of us naturally think of the ministry of the Word as work, feeling the burden and even scheduling time for sermon prep (2 Timothy 4:2). But how often do we feel a burden and actually schedule time to pray? Yet, the Bible marks out prayer as a clear expectation, alongside the private (think "counseling") and public (think "preaching") ministry of the Word. Charles Spurgeon says, "I know of no better thermometer to your spiritual temperature than this, the measure of the intensity of your prayer."[3]

So at the outset, note this expectation of Scripture: Pastors must guard space for study, preparation, prayer, and preaching/teaching.

2. Shepherding the flock personally

God expects pastors to serve not only as preachers but also personal shepherds (1 Peter 5:2–3). Often this entails listening to burdens, visiting the sick, counseling the hurting, discipling believers, correcting with gentleness, encouraging the weary, praying with members, and guiding them to glorify and enjoy God. Paul extends the point further when he urges elders to "be on guard for yourselves and for all the flock" (Acts 20:28). And perhaps we may find the greatest exhortation in the expectation of Jesus himself, spoken to Peter three times. In John's Gospel, Jesus tells Peter to "feed my sheep," an intimate, tender, and personal act of compassion and care (John 21:15–17).

God expects church leaders to spend time with people—listening, counseling, discipling, visiting, and knowing the sheep. The larger a church grows, the more easily this functional expectation may drift into the background. So a loving caution seems appropriate: Beware of seeing your church as a professional organization that can be led from the office. John Piper even warns us, "We pastors are being killed by the professionalizing of the pastoral ministry. The mentality of the professional is not the mentality of the prophet. Professionalism has nothing to do with the essence and heart of the Christian ministry."[4]

Remember, real shepherds do not have reclusive offices; or, rather, we might say the office of the shepherd exists in every field to which he leads the sheep. Of one thing we can be assured: The effective pastor often walks in the presence of the sheep. In our modern age, that means both physically and virtually, but the point stands. Scripture calls the shepherds of God's flock to a personal and personable life and ministry.

3. Equipping the saints for ministry

The personable office of pastor leads right into this next biblical expectation of time use. Why do you suppose God expects the shepherds to spend personal time with the sheep? We could list many reasons, but here's the primary answer given: God charges shepherds "to equip the saints for the work of ministry, to build up the body of Christ" (Ephesians 4:12). God's vision for his people does not include burdened-up and burned-out leaders who do all the ministry themselves, but instead leaders who invest their time and energy to equip others. Remember Paul's instruction to Timothy: "What you have heard from me . . . commit to faithful men who will be able to teach others also" (2 Timothy 2:2). The implication for shepherding time is that spiritual leaders will invest intentional time in training, discipling, and delegating—thereby multiplying ministry through others.

Ask the average pastor "How's the church?" and almost invariably you will hear a version of this answer: "Oh, busy, busy, busy." For most of us, no more honest answer can be given. Ministry often feels like an endless busyness. Productivity guru Cal Newport refers to this as the "hyperactive hivemind." Newport describes this mentality further: "We use visible activity as a crude proxy for actual productivity—if you can see me in my office . . . see my email replies and chat messages arriving regularly . . . then at the very least, you know I'm doing something."[5] The real question is not whether you are busy, but what you are busy with.

4. Guarding doctrine and refuting error

Next, we find that equipping the saints for the work of ministry includes more than delegation of tasks. It also includes spiritual equipping in the truth. A portion of a pastor's time must be devoted to strengthening believers to know the truth and discern error.

Paul wrote to Titus that an elder must hold "to the faithful message as taught, so that he will be able both to encourage with sound teaching and to refute those who contradict it" (Titus 1:9). This exhortation flowed out of the apostle Paul's actual life and ministry. Remember that Paul spent three years, night and day, tearfully warning his people of the error which could hinder their sanctification (Acts 20:29–32).

Here we find again a biblical expectation of time stewardship which requires study, discernment, and sometimes difficult conversations.

5. Modeling godly character

The daily life of a pastor comprises a large part of ministry, as well, especially as he leads by example. This marks another category of timely concern. A pastor working with the Fellowship of Christian Athletes made a statement I (Rush) have not forgotten in thirty years. He said, "People may refute what you say, but they will never refute how you live." Every Christian leader should emblazon this powerful injunction on his heart.

We invest loads of time in the preparation of our words, but comparatively little time goes into the cultivation of our character. Though it sounds strange, we find it true in our lives. Ministry can become so busy with good works that we neglect the weightier matters of our life and character. Thankfully, Scripture gives us solid direction on this point.

You will certainly recall Paul's explanation of pastoral qualifications to both Timothy and Titus (1 Timothy 3:1–7; Titus 1:5–9). The author of Hebrews instructs the believers to "Remember your leaders who have spoken God's word to you. As you carefully observe the outcome of their lives, imitate their faith" (Hebrews 13:7). How can Christians do this very thing unless the shepherds invest in their own holiness, marriages, families, and personal walks with Christ? You already know the answer. As coming chapters will cover, God expects you to apply some of your pastoral time to your own personal development.

6. Administering with wisdom and prudence

Okay, here comes the part you may least desire: administration. Our respective seminary class loads included a course called Administration and Education in the Local Church. Sounds *boooorrrinng*. The class covered things like church budgeting, execution of staff performance reviews, setting the church calendar, assimilating new members, blah, blah, blah. A few years later, the reality of church leadership hit hard, and many students changed their tunes.

Like it or not, God calls church leaders not only to provide a theological oversight but also to give wise attention to the orderly functioning of the church (1 Corinthians 14:40). We give thanks to the deacons for their important role in meeting the practical needs of the church, while allowing the ministry of the Word to move forward unhindered. And yet, this cannot happen without the elders' clear vision and practical attention to administrative direction. Even the incessant evangelist and apostle to the Gentiles cared about these matters. Recall how he instructed Titus to "set right what was left undone" and "appoint elders in every town," thereby highlighting the expectation of structured leadership and oversight (Titus 1:5).

Such careful administration demands the intentional use of time for planning, communication, delegation, and oversight, so the overall function of the church supports—rather than hinders—the central gospel ministry. Hear Richard Baxter on this matter: "The work of a minister is not only to preach, but to oversee the flock, to take heed to all the flock, and to the ordering of the affairs of the Church."[6] In this way, administration is the wise and prudent handmaiden of the central mission of every local church. Church leaders must certainly guard against the consuming potential of administrative details. At the same time, we cannot neglect this responsibility without the church falling into disorder or ineffectiveness.

7. Caring for one's family

Finally, and no less importantly, we must give unmistakable attention to the pastor's family. Scripture sets before every church leader a top-shelf expectation, and it has to do with your first and foremost responsibility: home. To care for the household of faith, pastors need to faithfully care for their own, literal households. Another biblical qualification of pastoral leadership chimes in here: "He must manage his own household competently and have his children under control with all dignity. (If anyone does not know how to manage his own household, how will he take care of God's church?)"

(1 Timothy 3:4–5). The health of a pastor's family is inseparable from his credibility and effectiveness in shepherding God's church. Before he can pastor the church, he must pastor his family, which often includes a wife and kids as the Lord gives blessing (Titus 1:6).

The grave danger and ease of home neglect is shocking. Take the example of Anglican cleric, theologian, evangelist, and cofounder of Methodism, John Wesley. For someone who accomplished so much good, his marriage was notoriously bad. He and his wife, Molly, relentlessly slung insults at each other at home. Their fights eventually spilled over into the public. He seemed to view Molly as a personal servant, while also lambasting her as rebellious. Though he left for gospel reasons, John was often away from home for months at a time, leaving Molly to tire of loneliness. Once, in 1758, John left for a preaching tour, parting from Molly with the insult, "I hope I shall see your wicked face no more."[7]

This story of John Wesley stands a far cry from Paul's instruction that husbands love their wives as Christ loved the church, and to shepherd their own children and households with nourishing and cherishing care (Ephesians 5:25; 6:4). Surely, Wesley felt the same pinch of limited time and high aspirations which every pastor feels. Yet the call remains to intentionally dedicate time to love, nurture, and lead our families. Neglecting one's marriage or children—the closest neighbors—in the name of ministry undercuts the gospel we cherish and proclaim. Faithful shepherding of God's flock begins with faithful shepherding of the smaller flock at home.

With those seven expectations in mind, we more clearly see how effective pastors need to not only identify but also shape the expectations placed upon their time. We can do so by recognizing, teaching, and modeling biblical expectations, while also keeping in view the personal, family, and cultural contexts in which the pastor life functions. Let's now consider ways to shape the time expectations of your church.

Shaping Cultural Time Expectations

Have you ever worn the wrong clothes to an event? You thought "business casual" meant shorts and flip-flops, and later realized it meant something embarrassingly different. Consider an unthinking CEO who pulls a suit from a discount store bin. He wears the suit to work, hoping it will increase his intimidation factor. Everyone in the office can tell it's a woman's pantsuit, with fluffy shoulder pads and a tailored fit. Though the CEO insists his suit is simply a European cut, he has unknowingly broken the cultural norms, creating confusion and inviting ridicule in the process.

> Faithful shepherding of God's flock begins with faithful shepherding at home.
>
> ~ ~ ~
>
> *Are you meeting the needs and expectations of your family in this season?*

The new pastor learns quickly that certain cultural expectations exist in every church, not only in the office but throughout the congregation. On his first Sunday, he preaches tie-less and khaki-ed to a crowd of furrowed brows and backhanded compliments about being "casual." He makes a phone call to a member in the hospital and learns the cultural expectation of in-person hospital visitation. He misses a committee meeting to make that important hospital visit but later hears "the pastors always attend these meetings." And these cultural faux pas do not only affect the uninitiated pastors among us; they affect even the veterans who have long served the church. What is one to do about this? We propose taking a three-fold approach to cultural expectations, especially related to ministry time.

First, take a listening tour by asking the key leaders and servants of the church to share their expectations of your pastoral time. Guessing at the cultural expectations will leave you groping in the dark. Leaning into assumptions won't help. Instead, pastors should open clear communication about what the sheep have come to expect and what has fashioned their culture of pastoral time. Not only will it help you establish a clear understanding, but you will find that consideration for others will build trust and comfort between you and your sheep.

Second, compile those insights into a journal or document so you will begin to see how those align with your own best rhythms and practices. You will also more clearly see how the culture of expectation might need gentle shaping through your careful leadership.[8] Some pastors feel stuck in the culture of their churches, as if nothing can be changed. Church culture is meant to be shaped, because failure to do so contributes to the high rate of burned-out, frustrated pastors.[9]

Third, as you compile the insights gained from open communication about pastoral expectations, consider your active and passive actions over the course of a week. Take inventory of your typical availability, response times, days of rest, and how you choose between the many ways you can use your time as a pastor. Find some points of tension where your best pastoral rhythms or functions conflict with the expectations of the congregation, as you've learned them on your listening tour. Consider how those intersections either reinforce or distract from the culture you are shepherding in your church.

The Beautiful Work of Culture-Shaping

Whatever you do, don't neglect this important aspect of church leadership. The matter cannot be overstated. Few things can shape the culture of your church like shepherding expectations on your pastoral ministry time. It will refine not only the congregation but also your life as a pastor in the church and as a leader in your home and community.

It would be foolish to impose personal and professional expectations on a community. It is just as irrational to allow your ministry to be ruled by unhelpful cultural expectations in the church, which then influence every area of life. The way of wisdom honors cultural expectations and thereby maximizes the supra-cultural truth of the gospel, creating realistic expectations that are recognizable and beneficial to the church. Because every church holds a unique culture, various time management books can be helpful, but they cannot simply plug and play as a guiding authority on how to manage time effectively. Remember this: You must always shepherd time locally. Trying to apply someone else's pastoral expectations on a macro level will invariably lead to miscommunication, confusion, and trouble.

> Few things can shape the culture of your church like shepherding expectations on your pastoral ministry time.
>
> ~ ~ ~
>
> *What are some active and passive ways you might begin to do this?*

Additionally, biblical principles and expectations regarding pastoral time are factors that shape the culture. There is a kind and beautiful work in recognizing and shaping a culture that reflects biblically-shaped expectations of pastoral time and applies to every ministry subculture you serve.

Reflection Questions

1. Have you unwittingly discovered expectations those in your church have for you (perhaps by failing to meet them and finding out later)? Go ahead and write them down.
2. What are the hardest biblical expectations for you to implement? Why is that?

3. Faithful shepherding of God's flock begins with faithful shepherding at home. Are you meeting the needs and expectations of your family in this season? If not, consider what might need to change.
4. What are some ways that your abiding in Christ helps to find the impact of unmet expectations?
5. Few things can shape the culture of your church like shepherding expectations on your pastoral ministry time. What are some active and passive ways you might begin to do this?

Action Step

Make a journal entry about your current perception of time within your pastoral role. Describe areas where you feel time is abundant versus scarce. Identify practical ways you can create more balance and intentionality in your schedule.

Chapter 4
Engaging Time Guilt

KYLE SITS AT his desk late at night. He stares into a life of overloaded meetings, unfinished sermons, unanswered emails, and unvisited sheep. Where has the time gone? His head drops to the desk. The clock ticks past midnight. He despairs, "I'll never catch up."

As Derek greets people after the service, a church member quietly says, "You know, Pastor, my dad spent last week in the hospital. I hoped you would visit him." A pit settles into Derek's stomach. In the hustle and bustle of daily life, he failed to remember this important hardship. No matter how many good things he accomplished, this one omission feels defeating. With defeat comes guilt and the sense that his stewardship of time never proves effective enough.

Time guilt looms over many pastors with a distracting power. This kind of guilt does not center simply on questions of busyness and logistics. It's a sense that one is failing his people and his God. In this chapter, the reality of guilt and its drain on us and our time comes into view.

As we considered in chapter 3, one reality of pastoral ministry is the tension created by perceived unmet expectations from someone in the congregation, family, local community, or even yourself. On our best days, we lean into the passionate fulfillment of our pastoral callings. But what happens when, despite our best efforts, we still miss the mark? What do you do when feelings of guilt pull you back from your best ministry efforts? How do you handle the very real experience of pastoral time guilt?

For many, time guilt looms like a low-grade fever. It's never fully debilitating, but always just under the surface. Do you remember the *Peanuts* character Pig-Pen, always surrounded by a cloud of dust?[1] Like Pig-Pen's dust cloud, time guilt hangs around pastors, following them into every setting. In this way, guilt can drain our pastoral powers, leaving us less effective than we otherwise could be. For pastors, the word *guilt* can carry several different meanings, and if we don't sort them out carefully, we will apply the wrong medicine to our souls.

Two Kinds of Guilt

At its root, guilt is the sense of failing to meet a standard. For pastors, that standard often feels impossibly high. Pride can feed into this struggle, because we imagine ourselves capable of doing more, being more, and pleasing everyone at once. In truth, we are limited. We cannot do everything. We cannot be everywhere. And we must not let guilt press us into measuring our worth by our output.

Make no mistake, complex challenges surround the experience of guilt. Therefore, we must learn to diagnose guilt as carefully as a cardiologist diagnoses the heart. Like many topics, the subject of guilt contains the propensity to collapse any related question or experience under that one complicated word. Thankfully, the Bible gives us nuances and categories so we can properly diagnose and respond to the actual reality.

Richard Baxter exhorts his readers to "spend your time in nothing which you know must be repented of; in nothing which you could not pray for a blessing upon; in nothing which you could not review with a quiet conscience on your dying bed; in nothing which you would not be found doing if death should surprise you in the act."[2]

At the most basic level, pastoral guilt falls into two categories: true guilt and false guilt. True guilt is exactly what it sounds like—a genuine sense of conviction over real sin or genuine failures of stewardship before God. False guilt, by contrast, is the feeling of having failed even when no actual sin or unfaithfulness is present. Both experiences are real. Both demand a response. But they require very different medicine. Learning to tell them apart is one of the most important skills a pastor can develop.

True Guilt and How It Manifests

Sometimes guilt comes honestly—a true sense of conviction of sin before God. We see how time has been squandered, responsibilities neglected, and selfishness has been allowed to dictate our choices. No pastor can live peacefully under the constant pressure of guilt and still invest himself in joyful, effective ministry.

It is worth noting that true guilt is not always the same in its character. Scripture distinguishes between sins of commission and sins of ignorance—intentional and unintentional sins. In Leviticus 4, we learn the key difference. Unintentional sins are committed out of ignorance, negligence, or weakness—not out of a deliberate heart of rebellion or irresponsibility. In our context, it means that even pastors sometimes don't realize their error, or that we may fail in a way that's not purely willful. In his Word, God acknowledges our human frailty and offers in Christ the way for restoration and change.

On the other hand, we all know the sting of intentional or defiant sins, which are committed knowingly, deliberately, and with a kind of "high hand" (to use the phrase from

Numbers 15:30 ESV).[3] We can be aware of God's law and disregard it. The difference is not merely about the size of the sin but about the heart posture. An unintentional sin is weakness under God's authority; an intentional sin is open defiance against his authority. Both are real failures that need God's grace and mercy, but the pastoral experience in each differs.

> Pastoral guilt falls into two categories: true guilt and false guilt.
>
> ~ ~ ~
>
> *Can you identify a recent experience of each one?*

A pastor who knowingly neglects the careful use of his time is guilty in a different way than a pastor who, out of inexperience, weakness, or overwhelm, fails to steward time wisely. In either case, the guilt is real—it simply varies in degree.

One of the immense blessings which come to us through Jesus's gracious acceptance is the ability, with hope, to look our failures directly in the face. And since we have this bright gospel blessing illuminating the way, we can turn up the heat on this topic of time guilt. Though it likely will sting, consider eight ways pastors misuse time. Ready?

1. Social media crusades and digital distractions

Yes, it's an easy but necessary target. You need not look further than YouTube to see the endless threads of online pastoral and political disputes. A recent study shows the average person engages social media two and a half hours per day across seven different platforms.[4] Since digitally engaged pastors follow hundreds of church members (beyond the usual accounts), we assume the social media problem to be even worse for them. When the average pastor spends two and a half hours each day on social media, the cumulative investment rivals the hours of a part-time job—effectively rendering them pseudo-bivocational, laboring not only in the church but also in the endless digital marketplace of attention. It should not be this way.

How much otherwise productive time are pastors losing through reading, scrolling, commenting, debating, and engaging in online activities which amount to little real value? We will give more detailed advice later in the book about how to redeem the time by eliminating nearly all social media use.

2. Living in the inbox

In this modern age, life not only requires email use, but many pastors (and everyday people, for that matter) simply can't get it under control. Look at your inbox now. If you see more than fifteen messages awaiting your attention, you have a problem. And if you have opened the email app more than three times already today, you have an even bigger problem.

The inbox poses a big problem for pastors and their stewardship of time. The way many of us handle the inbox ends up wasting our time more than redeeming it. You may not realize that it's okay to be bad at email. Many of us feel pressure to be good at email, but we erroneously think being good at it means being highly engaged with it. That's wrong thinking, and later we'll help you get a grip on it.

3. Overcommitting to meetings

Meetings are a good fuel of ministry. Think of all the different kinds of meetings. Elder meetings. Deacon meetings. Discipleship meetings. Committee meetings. Denominational meetings. Counseling meetings. Community meetings. But like many other areas of life, too much of a good thing is a bad thing. Certainly, it's true of meetings. Most of us make the mistake of attending or leading every meeting—often without an agenda or clear purpose. We do this out of habit, obligation, or fear of disappointing others. We end up stressing and feeling guilty about all the unfinished business left in the wake of endless (and often unnecessary) meetings.

4. Neglecting delegation

Many pastors try to do everything themselves—administration, tech, maintenance—instead of equipping and empowering the body to serve. Yet many pastors live as if time grows on trees. Although we know time is a limited commodity, our lives suggest the contrary when we stack task upon task. But there are simply more possible tasks than hours in the day. The "do it all" approach results in many of the most important tasks remaining undone as we race against a relentless clock. Why does this happen? A failure to delegate.

5. Substituting administration for discipleship

Often an amnesia of calling accompanies the neglect of delegation. Despite the clear pastoral mission and duties laid out in Scripture, we are all prone to forget our main purposes in God's kingdom. Specifically, the line between the offices of pastor/elder and deacon becomes blurred. Pastors, then, lose precious pastoral time carrying out the important work which should belong to deacons, spending more time on forms, policies, and logistics than in prayer, teaching, evangelism, and soul care (Acts 6:1–7).

6. Failing to guard personal devotion

This one might sting, and it should. We've felt the pangs of time guilt often as we let our personal relationship time with God fall to the wayside. The pressures and responsibilities of ministry have a strange way of seducing pastors into believing the outward work of ministry pleases God more than the inward work of the Spirit in us. We allow good things like sermon prep and vision-casting to crowd out personal Bible reading and prayer, starving the one soul that's responsible to care for the many. This might be the most important reason of all to shepherd our time well.

7. Avoiding hard conversations

Time guilt can rise from not only the amount of time we dedicate to a given task but also the kind of time to which we give our attention. No pastor enjoys the hard conversations which arise in every healthy church. We find ourselves delaying difficult but necessary moments with struggling members, leaders, or families. The desire to avoid discomfort, hoping the problems will just disappear on their own, ends up making problems worse and draining more time later. And what do we often feel along with the loss of time? Guilt.

8. Insecurity and comparison

Finally, we waste emotional energy measuring our ministry against other pastors or churches rather than faithfully tending the flock God has entrusted to us. It is unhelpful and unhealthy to measure our success or faithfulness against what God is doing somewhere else, rather than taking stock of what God has asked us to do where we are and making sure we are staying on course.

False Guilt and How It Manifests

At other times, what we call guilt is actually legalism dressed up as piety. We know that forgiveness is in Christ, yet we secretly insist that we must do something more—suffer enough, feel badly enough, or accomplish enough ministry to earn God's favor. Paul makes this precise distinction between the true shepherds and the false teachers around Philippi. He warns against the dogs, the evil workers, who mutilate the flesh, rather than boasting in Christ (Philippians 3:2–3).

Biblical counselor Ed Welch put it this way:

> Practitioners know that there is forgiveness of sins through Jesus, but they attach a rider to forgiveness that says they need to do something to earn it, such as feel really, really bad, or reform themselves before they receive forgiveness. This version of guilt puts a human face on the Lord and essentially says, "There is no such thing as a free lunch. If I have sinned, I have to make restitution in order to make it up to you."[5]

It's like trying to clean the house before the maid arrives.

Still other moments reveal that our guilt grows in the soil of shame. We feel exposed, judged, or inadequate because our ministry efforts have not borne fruit in keeping with expectations. Or the shame we feel does not connect to actual sin at all, but to our weakness as mere creatures—the limits of our natural finitude. Shame whispers, "You're a failure. You'll never measure up." But it is not the voice of the Shepherd. To confuse shame with true guilt only deepens our frustration.

Another layer emerges when we submit ourselves to the opinions of others. Pastors, perhaps more than most, live under a constant sense of scrutiny. If a member is displeased or disappointed, we instinctively feel we have failed—even when no sin is present. This is where fear of man masquerades as guilt. It steals joy and burdens ministry with impossible expectations.

And finally, some guilt is simply the result of being human. We cannot predict every crisis, make every visit, or anticipate every need. We remain forever finite creatures, not omniscient shepherds.

False guilt shows up in the most ordinary places. Take something as ordinary as a vacation. Many pastors feel a twinge of guilt for stepping away, even though God offers and commands rest (Mark 6:31). Or consider the purchase of an enjoyable but necessary item, something like a reliable car or a smart watch. Since the generosity of church members provides a pastor's salary, feelings of guilt can arise whenever his spending moves beyond what others are able to spend.

> We cannot predict every crisis, make every visit, or anticipate every need.
>
> ~ ~ ~
>
> *What are some internal expectations you place on yourself that are actually beyond your capacities?*

Sometimes false guilt surfaces around family issues. Have you felt guilty when your wife or children lack your level of enthusiasm for ministry? You might be tempted to think this reflects poorly on your leadership or faithfulness. Then, add in a whopping sense of the undone. There are always people to visit, additional study you could do, extra church programs waiting to launch, leaders to train, problems to solve. The undone is never done, and it brings a nagging subcutaneous guilt—like a low-grade fever that never breaks. We sometimes feel this guilt hanging over our rest and renewal, whispering to us in the night, "Shouldn't you be writing that sermon, meeting that member, catching up on those emails?" Even time at home with family or friends can feel suspect, as though enjoying life betrays a true commitment to the church.

False guilt rises from the gap between pastoral ambition and creaturely limitations. We've noticed pastors possess a natural drive. We all long to see the kingdom advanced, our churches grow, and God's people flourish in his gospel blessings. Even still, more can always be done. The temptation, then, is to interpret our human finiteness as a form of unfaithfulness. In the tyrannical voice of the undone, we wrongly conclude, "If I were more spiritual, more disciplined, more selfless, I would ____________." This is a prime example of false guilt. God calls his pastoral people (and all people) to faithfulness, not omnipotence. He calls us to steward our limits as much as our gifts.

Gospel Remedies for True and False Guilt

Recognizing these distinctions changes the way we respond to time guilt. Instead of carrying every burden as if it were the same, we learn to apply the gospel with precision. True guilt calls for repentance and faith; for resting in Christ's finished work. Shame calls for hearing the Lord's welcome. Fear of man calls for fearing the Lord above all else. And human limitation calls for humility and dependence.

Still, the pastor's struggle is real. We may feel guilty for time spent on activities not immediately visible as ministry—recreation, physical rest, literature, a concert, woodworking, lunches with family. We may also feel guilty when ministry outcomes fall short: "I could have studied more." "That meeting wasn't what it needed to be." "I'm falling behind in administration." To shepherd our time well, we must distinguish between guilt that stems from true sin or poor stewardship, and guilt that simply reflects our limitations or points to improper expectations.

Here is where faithfulness reframes the whole conversation. We cannot define success in ministry as the ability to meet every expectation, but rather to shepherd expectations in a way that leads us toward pastoral discipline. In God's economy, faithfulness equals success. In our own ministries, we often found ourselves discouraged not because we were wildly unfaithful, but because we placed fear of people before God's covenant love. Fear of man made others big and God small.

Learning to confess that fear and serve people in love has been a slow but freeing lesson.

Together, with the help of Christ and his people, we can learn to steward both time and guilt in a way that strengthens ministry rather than weakens it.

Live out of your identity in Christ

The value of pastors is not in what they do but who they are in Christ. Reframing pastoral expectations and identifying the nature of the guilt that can seep into the heart of the pastor is the best way to engage with the guilt we feel. As we understand that Jesus has borne all our guilt and that we can rightly and joyfully serve him not out of duty but delight, it allows us not to ignore our guilt or pass it through deeds, but to engage with it rightfully and to live accurately out of it.

> We remain forever finite creatures, not omniscient shepherds.
>
> ~ ~ ~
>
> *Because you want to be a good pastor, what are some internal pressures or expectations you place on yourself that are actually beyond your capacities?*

Many pastors are dealing with guilt because they have not been able to clearly define the expectations of their role and season of ministry and life. To address guilt is to identify how it expresses a fundamental understanding of how time is used. Motivating guilt moves against the motivating work of pastoral ministry of the gospel. The message of identity, help, and hope of the gospel for others to release their guilt is the same for the ministers themselves. Guilt might look different, but it is similar to the struggles of others.

Know your limits

Everyone has a threshold of service. This is the internal category that you naturally serve and minister into. This could be reflected in your personality, strengths, or weaknesses. In essence, you already have a framework for how you view your time as a pastor. This could be from contexts you have served or people in your life. We have found that many of our expectations of shepherding time are subjective and influenced more by relationships and experiences than by biblical principles. The point here is to have an honest consideration of your own expectations of your time as a pastor. Where are your gaps or nonnegotiables? How are those related to biblical principles?

We have found that pastors are the most critical of themselves and think they can do more than they should or are able to. Consider what is not only aspirational but also realistic in how to shepherd your time for God's glory.

Prepare for when guilt strikes

Pastors do not react to guilt but respond to it. This means that pastors must prepare before guilt strikes to respond to it rightly. This means having regular rhythms of identifying where the root heart issue of their guilt is found and engaging it with the gospel. Having a plan for when guilty feelings strike helps you discern the difference between genuine and misplaced guilt. Mark and remember these powerful words from Martin Luther: "When the devil throws your sins in your face and declares that you deserve death and hell, tell him this: 'I admit that I deserve death and hell. What of it? For I know One who suffered and made satisfaction on my behalf. His name is Jesus Christ, Son of God, and where He is, there I shall be also.'"[6]

Identify those who can support you

Even on our best days, we cannot manage guilt on our own. Pastors need community as much as those whom we seek to care for. Welcome in leadership and trusted friends to help you accurately address and thoughtfully manage guilt as it strikes.

A word of caution. Pastors who are motivated by guilt are bound to burn out. It is unsustainable to set the pace of ministry by trying to be good enough. Jesus is enough, and we are his faithful under-shepherds. Considering how much time and what kind of time you give to guilt in your life is going to transform your weekends, both Saturday and Sunday.

Together, with the help of Christ and his people, we can learn to steward both time and guilt in a way that strengthens ministry rather than weakens it.

Reflection Questions

1. Can you identify a recent experience of true guilt—an actual failure in your stewardship of time or your calling? How did you respond to it?
2. Can you identify a recent experience of false guilt—a feeling of failure that was not rooted in actual sin? Where did it come from? Was it legalism, shame, fear of man, or simply the weight of human limitation?
3. What are some internal expectations you place on yourself that are actually beyond your capacities? How can you shepherd your time with more realistic expectations of yourself?
4. What are some common ways you try to deal with feelings of guilt in your life? How do those strategies relate to the gospel?
5. How does the gospel bring a strong sense of freedom from guilt to your ministry?

Action Step

Write down three things you currently feel guilty about in your ministry. For each one, ask: Is this true guilt (a real failure of stewardship or sin) or false guilt (an unrealistic expectation, a fear of man, or simply the weight of being finite)? Then, write one gospel truth that speaks directly to each item. At the end of the week, reflect on how this exercise changed the way you approached your time and your calling.

Chapter 5

Recognizing Time Thieves

TIME THIEVES LURK around every corner. The nature of "on-call" pastoral ministry—happily making yourself available to parishioners—presents incredible potential for interruption and redirection at almost any moment. The focused pastor must, then, develop a flexible plan for handling interruptions in a way which incorporates them into the flow of busy ministry life. He must not allow interruptions to steal time from the essential tasks of caring for his church, family, and other responsibilities (Colossians 4:5).

It is interesting that we feel unproductive and ineffective when we don't complete tasks on our list because of interruptions. But when we look back on the day, we find numerous reasons to rejoice over good gospel ministry. In guarding against time thieves, we aim to foil common thieves and reinvest in ministry. Time thieves, as we are calling them here, sneak up on us. As we consider their role in shepherding time, remember these *thieves* do not necessarily represent bad things which should be avoided but also good things which pop up and interfere with our plans. We want to become students of these important factors of shepherding time.

This craft of shepherding time thieves is an essential ability that every pastor discovers. We must learn to engage in the parking lot conversation, take the phone call on our day off, and especially care for the intrusive moments and mindless texts that arrive in the middle of the staff meeting. All of us need help with the simple and real distractions, and with some principles in place, we can get a handle on them. Cotton Mather insists, "Redeem this time to your own advantage, to the best advantage."[1]

As we considered earlier, a shepherd's time contains his most valuable commodity. Thus, we minister time. We proctor time. Do you remember taking the SAT or ACT in high school? As his or her main responsibility, the proctor watched the clock. What does that title mean? Well, readers who love Latin will enjoy learning the word *proctor* comes from the prefix *pro*, which means "on behalf of." The prefix combines with the root *curare*, which means "to take care." Put it together and we define a proctor as someone who takes care on behalf of another. What an important title for pastors to embrace. We serve as caretakers of time on behalf of others. Everything we do with our time serves or neglects the good of others. For this reason, we press upon you the importance of guarding your time and the spiritual consequences it carries in the lives of others.

The act of shepherding happens in the context of time. Like a bicycle left on a busy street with no lock, the pastor's time can be stolen away by a number of thieves who regularly pass by. And perhaps the most tragic fact about time thieves is that once time is stolen, we can never get it back. This presents us with even more reason to consider some of the most wanted time thieves. We'll consider four types of time thieves: distracted time, disruptive time, demanding time, and destructive time.

Distracted Time

Most people have a love-hate relationship with cats. They present themselves as warm, snuggly creatures, but when you look away the cats will play. And not just play, but they will scratch up your couch, eat your snacks, and rub their fine hairs into your nice suit. Cats are an exercise in contradictions.

The only redeeming quality among cats is, perhaps, their curiosity. And yet, we've all heard it said, "Curiosity killed the cat." Leave it to cats to take something good like curiosity and turn it for evil. Despite our disfavor for cats, we'd like to use them for good in just this one case as we consider the first time thief: distraction.

> Once time is stolen, we can never get it back.
>
> ~ ~ ~
>
> *What have you lost to unprotected time?*

Curiosity proves one of the best and yet most troubling qualities of the average pastor. His curiosity moves him to explore people, ideas, Scripture, politics, and the wider world. That curious instinct fuels learning, sermon depth, and empathy for the weak and sinners. However, we must acknowledge the shadow side. The same curious leadings which produce bright ministry can also fragment our focus, making us subservient to every interesting thought.

Be honest, dear brothers: countless times you have chased down miles of grammatical road for some obscure Greek word. You have researched the origins of bewildering cultural trends, peered into the tabloid lives of celebrities, and analyzed the social media algorithm in hopes of breaking forth an internet revival. Wait, is that just us? No, you too, friends. And in those moments, we neglected the weightier provisions of our calling.

Now, let's be clear. Most of these curious distractions do not betray an unrighteous root within. They distract not with sinful curiosity but an unfocused kind—a neglectful kind, an unhelpful kind. They steal away the precious funds of time we could spend in higher pursuits.

Distractions work quietly in the background. Over time they pile up into a time deficit or debt which becomes hard to overcome. Distractions do the work of a pickpocket who slips by you on a busy street, and not like the bank robber who announces his heist with shots in the air. These distractions come in the form of unnecessary conversations, hobby-related research, digital drift, endless email loops. The list could go on and on. Becoming alert to this time thief helps us avoid it.

The problem with distraction does not come from outside of us but wells up from the inside. Distraction not only hinders our work but often reveals misplaced wants—ruling desires for comfort, novelty, or approval more than fruitfulness. Recognizing this will help us capture and convict the time thief of distraction. Ask yourself this question during your personal distractions: "What does this distraction promise me right now which I value more than Christ's call to faithfulness?" Unclutter your mind and train your eyes to look out upon the pasture of your calling. Find those lurking distractions which make promises they cannot keep.

Disruptive Time

The pastor's life unfolds among people, not in the sterile, tightly controlled spaces of a perfect world. The shepherd's work among sheep entails disruption and inconvenience. Sheep are sheep, and the field is beset with myriad intrusions. We've noted the problem with distraction, namely its self-inflicted nature due to the wandering impulses within our hearts. The next time thief—disruption—stands in distinction. Disruptions intrude upon us from the outside. They pose a different, serious challenge to our ability to shepherd time.

Furthermore, unlike many of the trivial *distractions* we face, *disruptions* still present important opportunities for ministry. A hospital call, a member in crisis, an unexpected funeral, a last-minute counseling need, one of your children becomes sick at school. We cannot and should not cast away these disruptions. They belong to the realm of ministry in many cases. Yet still, they have the power to disrupt best laid plans and steal away time.

Another danger lies within the challenge of disruptions. We must not resent them or fail to adapt when they press upon us. Instead, we can see them as pivots to be made. The key insight we want to present at this point reminds us that faithful ministry requires flexibility.

Anyone in youth ministry (or any ministry for that matter) knows well that great truth of the universe: Murphy's Law. The law's roots reach back to aerospace engineer, Edward A. Murphy Jr. In 1949, Murphy studied human tolerance of acceleration and deceleration—that is, g-force resistance—for those uninitiated with high-powered jets. During one such test, an electrical technician wired sensors incorrectly. Murphy remarked in frustration, "If there's any way to do it wrong, he'll find it." His words later came into common parlance as, "If anything can go wrong, it will."[2] Have truer words been spoken?

Thus, wise shepherding of time requires a robust appreciation for our stewardship amid God's sovereignty. Pastor John Flavel insists, "The providence of God never mistakes, nor does it ever miss its aim."[3] Many times we find divine appointments come at inopportune times. But when they arrive, the divine purposes within them remain intact. We can know that God ordains interruptions for our maturity and ministry.

Think of Jesus, who often faced disruptions. It seems he never met a disruption he didn't like. Whether blind men cried out from the side of the road (Mark 10:46–52), or children rushed up to greet him (Luke 18:15–17), or a woman desperate for healing pulled upon his robe (Mark 5:25–34), or a paralytic literally descends from above (Mark 2:1–12), we never find Jesus hurried or resentful.

Learning from Christ in the school of distraction teaches us that a pastor's calendar serves in an ever-disrupted mission. It must not direct and not enslave the pastor. Disruptions enter inevitably. In the coming pages, we will consider more practical guidance on rebuilding time stolen through the intrusive disruptions of life and ministry. We will see that even lost time can be redeemed when surrendered to the Chief Shepherd.

Demanding Time

Who knew sheep would be so demanding? We all enter ministry life with a touch of naïveté. To say we knew exactly what we were getting ourselves into would be far from the truth. We had a sense but not the whole picture. And yet, we should've known sheep work would make big demands on the time of shepherds. After all, we too are sheep.

The longer we spend in ministry, the more we understand pastoring comes with endless demands. As we acknowledged earlier, expectations abound. And yet we know many of the expectations held by church members are perfectly fair and important. In fact, it is quite good for the flock to expect their shepherd to be present and active in their lives. If they didn't expect this, it would signal a real mark of unhealthy church life. We have the expected privilege of personal presence in both celebration and crisis. What a good thing!

Like all good things in this fallen world, there's a catch. While many expectations felt by pastors are right and good, they also are demanding. They shape the rhythm of the pastor's time.

Take, for example, the emotional and logistical weight of basic pastoral counseling. Think about the way this single aspect of ministry evolves. With each instance, we must give ourselves first to preparation, then to the act of counseling, then to follow-up, then to debriefing, then we move into ongoing care. And the cycle repeats again. Multiply this by numerous needful sheep and the demands on time pile up, up, up.

To make matters more complicated, this same kind of cycle occurs around weddings, funerals, hospital visits, seasonal ministry changes, and more. Together, these demands touch upon every category of a pastor's time.

> It is good for the flock to expect their shepherd to be present and active in their lives.
>
> ~ ~ ~
>
> *Are there reasonable congregational expectations you haven't been able to meet in this way because of these time thieves?*

And you may have noticed, we haven't even considered the cycle of Sunday ministry responsibilities. Do you recall the famous sermon given by the powerful preacher S. M. Lockridge called "It's Friday, but Sunday's Coming"?[4] He explores the passion week of Jesus, noting at every turn that *Sunday's coming*. This message could easily describe every pastor's life week in and week out. Demands abound and still Sunday's coming. Rather than instill encouragement, for many of us, this reality can feel overwhelming.

Finally, we should add one more real demand on the pastor's time—ministry to his own family. In fact, this area of life presents not only a demand but a requirement of concern and dedication of time. The Scriptures clearly teach a pastor must care for his own household (1 Timothy 3:4–5).

We can see at least two reasons this reality can be difficult to handle.

First, faithful family life is part of faithful ministry. The pastor's home serves both as a place for rest and as an extension of ministry. Every pastor, then, lives a bit like the classic, old shopkeeper who lived above his store. Personal life of house and home melds with ministry life of church and flock. What a unique reality we navigate.

Second, the family dynamic brings a sense in which one remains "off duty" yet always available. Dear fellow pastor, keep in mind this is a feature and not a bug. While our families come with their own demands, they are not distractions.

Here's the ultimate reality: The shepherd who doesn't learn to engage wisely with these demands will soon serve them instead of Christ. But we can and must learn to guard our time with humility and the help of others. That's why we're glad you're reading this book. We feel the same demanding challenges and want to grow together in watchfulness.

Amid these demands, we can offer one central promise of good news: When the local church shepherd entrusts his life and time to Christ, and with humility invites the help he needs to guard it, the very demands which were so heavy will transform into the gracious joys which make ministry a delight. Remember the Prince of Preachers, Charles Spurgeon, who said, "If we bear no burdens but His burdens, and do no service but His service, then we shall find that His yoke is easy and His burden is light."[5]

Destructive Time

Wouldn't it be nice if an alarm existed which would alert us when a time thief is creeping in to steal away precious time? It would blare the siren all the time. We cannot leave the discussion of time thieves without acknowledging the destructive kind.

At this point, we need to direct focus again from the thieves outside of us to the thieves inside of us. The most destructive time thieves live in the hidden recesses of our own hearts. Truly, one could write endless books about the many destructive forces which emanate from our inner selves.

Cue John Calvin's Genevan voice echoing, "Man's nature, so to speak, is a perpetual factory of idols."[6] Thus, we ought to expect the most destructive time thieves swim in our hearts.

Think simply about the time each of us loses through our thought lives. We care deeply about the people of our churches and the health and effectiveness of ministry. However, even with such caring intentions can lurk the potential to spend countless hours thinking, replaying, or brooding over issues in the church. We shudder to think of how much good and joyful time we've both lost rehashing old conversations or imagined offenses, what one pastor we know called "vain imaginations."

How many days or months have we lost by worrying about the approval or disapproval of others, called in Scripture the "fear of mankind" (Proverbs 29:25)? Jesus himself warned us about such worry by asking the striking question, "Can any of you add one moment to his life span?" (Matthew 6:27). Quite the opposite happens; we deduct time.

The stress imposed by such undisciplined thinking may feel pastoral, but in reality, it produces little true benefit to your family or the kingdom. Destructive time thieves like brooding and worry do not amount to quality ministry but only mental and spiritual quicksand. As we become stuck in the quicksand of negative and unproductive thinking, sinful accommodation follows. We begin to make conscious trade-offs in the process, in the name of minor, excusable, or respectable time thieves.

We think things like, *I really do need to spend some time with the Lord in prayer, but ministry is just so busy right now.* Or perhaps you've heard this one bouncing around in your heart: *I'll only watch one episode because I just need a break.* It seems like a harmless accommodation, but what does it really accomplish? You don't gain the rest you need, and ministry goes unmet. Or finally, you may notice the small sense of irritation toward that difficult church member translates to neglect in the name of "being realistic" about his or her ability to change.

In reality, we should see ourselves as those in need of the greatest amount of change, and these destructive time thieves tell the tale. Jerry Bridges's words from *Respectable Sins* apply here:

> It's not enough to agree that we do tolerate at least some of them. Anyone except for the most self-righteous person will acknowledge that. "After all, no one is perfect," may be our attitude. But to honestly face those sins is another matter. For one thing, it is quite humbling. It also implies that we must do something about them. We can no longer continue to ignore them as we have in the past.[7]

Did you hear the accommodations built into this kind of thinking?

The greatest disqualifying acts in pastoral human history started as small tolerated and respectable excuses. Think back upon the public collapses we've witnessed from pastors in recent years. Every public collapse began as a private accommodation borne in the heart of destructive thoughts. Yikes! That probably sounds a little strong for a book about time management. Yet the point stands. If we are true shepherds of time, we must not treat the little moments as harmless discrepancies. Rather they inhabit our most precious commodity, which should be spent wisely on our true Shepherd and the sheep of his pasture (Psalm 95:6–7).

Reflection Questions

1. What time thief has stolen the most of your time?
2. What are some of the implications of these time thieves on your life?
3. Once time is stolen, we can never get it back. What have you lost to unprotected time? How can considering these losses motivate actions to keep time thieves away?
4. Think about practical steps you can take to guard against distractions. What are one or two things you can put in place right away?
5. Are there reasonable congregational expectations you haven't been able to meet because of these time thieves?

Action Step

Identify three major time thieves in your life. Create a strategy for each on how to avoid or mitigate their impact moving forward. Track your progress in avoiding these distractions over the next month.

Chapter 6
Mastering Time Pivots

LIVING AS A shepherd of people means giving thoughtful effort to everything in life for God's glory. This means seeing time as the context in which to live out our humanness and our vocational calling to make and multiply Christ-followers. Every moment in time holds incredible spiritual potential. There is no amoral time.

An inherent tension exists in pastoral ministry. Pastors have received a passionate call. To give one's whole life to the work of gospel ministry brings a good and consuming desire. But at times, you feel the tension between a desire for great ministry and the real limitations of time available to see that passion realized in fruitful ministry efforts. This can translate into frustration, depression, and, at times, guilt or exhaustion (as considered above).

We can all force ourselves to spend more time in study, more time in prayer, more time investing in family, more time in the counseling chair, more time in rest and reflection, more time planning for the future, more time to reach the unreached people groups. Pastoral time is time always in tension. The answer is not to find a way to release those tensions but to shepherd those tensions into a place of faith and flourishing (Romans 12:2).

Remember, the average pastor has upwards of 120 waking hours every week (depending on sleep habits)—120 hours!

No matter how big your church or how heavy your responsibilities, 120 hours is a load of time at your disposal. There is, in fact, enough time for family, ministry, rest, and even some additional outlets for impact on the side. We just need to get a better grip on those hours to make them count in better ways—better for us, for our people, and for the King and kingdom we love to serve.

Shepherding time as pastors presents a complicated set of challenges. We need an uncommon level of focus, perspective, and structure to handle the tension of our pastoral time. In light of this, let's consider how pastors can pivot with the need of the moment.

Pivoting in Time

Every pastor possesses a unique and dangerous skill set: the ability to pivot in time. On any given day, a pastor will encounter all kinds of information, circumstances, and personalities, many of which run back-to-back. *Pivoting* describes a quick redirection of attention from one kind of time to another. You experience this on afternoons in which different meetings or phone calls send you from place to place. Effectiveness at shepherding time requires this ability to pivot smoothly. This feature of pastoral ministry becomes particularly important when transitioning from church work to home life, requiring a focused and intentional pivot of care without distraction from the day's earlier events. To some, this might seem akin to unhealthy compartmentalization, but if theologically rooted and lovingly applied, a pastor must learn to thoughtfully navigate the various time demands throughout the day without going mad.

Puritan Thomas Watson emphasized the spiritual violence which appropriately applies to the kingdom of God. "The kingdom of heaven suffereth violence, and the violent take it by force. None get to heaven without violence. None are saved but those who labor and strive to enter in."[1] Watson means to point out that the Christian life is a spiritual war, which requires seriousness. We draw from this truth the serious role pastors play in that spiritual war. Thus, the pastor's ability to handle time, pivoting when needed, accounts for a key to their faithful fight.

The rightly developed skills of pastors allow them to serve the church as an imposing danger to forces of evil: the world, the flesh, and the devil. Truly, the value of rightly shepherding our time—in part, through a keen ability to flex and pivot with the demands of ministry—prepares pastors to serve well in the battle between two kingdoms, one of light and one of darkness. This provides just one reason why we're thinking carefully together about shepherding time.

Time doesn't shepherd itself. The pastor can become a skilled navigator of time or suffer under its oppressive rule. This chapter will orient us to the kinds of time every pastor must readily face. This takes into account how the shepherd understands and functions within the unique role, responsibility, and relationship of the situation he engages. We must recognize that any of those dynamics could change at a moment's notice, affecting the whole experience of a ministry day. We often find that effective gospel ministry is not a matter of content but of context. This chapter will help you see yourself in context and shape your effectiveness in each ministry component and the whole.

Readiness

One of the great examples of time-honoring readiness comes from a seventeenth-century Carmelite brother named Nicolas Herman. He spent his days in a Parisian monastery, not as a monk but as a lay brother. As his main assignment, he labored in the kitchen and repaired shoes. After his death, Joseph de Beaufort compiled a number of Herman's letters, writings, and other correspondence into a book called *The Practice of the Presence of God*.[2] More famously known as Brother Lawrence, Nicolas Herman's thoughts reveal a man ever ready to use time to the Lord's advantage.

He understood the important truth that time doesn't merely pass by us. Instead, time presents a context which every pastor inhabits. Many of us allow time to pass by with little thought. Not Brother Lawrence. He aimed to inhabit all kinds of time with the same serious focus. Listen to his words: "The time of business does not with me differ from the time of prayer; and in the noise and clatter of my kitchen. I possess God in as great tranquillity as if I were upon my knees."[3] The book brilliantly highlights the importance of pastoral readiness.

Every pastor inhabits time, but not every pastor does so with readiness. Ask yourself, "What kind of time do I inhabit right now?" Of course, in this moment you inhabit "reading time." And with that thought in mind, how focused are you as you read this book? Are you simply scanning the lines to get through this page? Are you reading with readiness, anticipating what might be gained between here and the close of this chapter?

You see, faithful pastors do not scan the timeline of their days simply to reach the end. They engage with the present moment according to a readied anticipation of ministry—like Brother Lawrence.

Younger pastors (and the older brother, for that matter) must come to see from experience that understanding his context and capacities presents a difficult but worthy challenge. It requires him to become a student of time with a keen and readied discipline to make the most of the time and talents

God has given. He cannot fully grasp the value of time by simply installing an app or buying a time-block calendar. True stewardship requires a commitment to study time and pivot according to the need of the moment. We need more than a plan. We need a reformation of time-readiness.

Consider the roles a shepherd plays in everyday life. These roles emerge in family life, ethnicity, relationships with neighbors, citizenship, church membership, vocational ministry, engaging with strangers, making acquaintances, and being a friend. One of the keys to readiness comes through seeing your primary role and place in the world you inhabit as that of a Christ-follower. It shapes all the other roles accordingly. Over the years, some pastors have engaged in their roles without a clear awareness of their primary role. This always leads to hardship and difficulty. The joy of knowing Christ brings to us the assurance that the role of believer stands supreme above all others. And that main covenant relationship empowers you to pivot gracefully the many other roles entrusted to you. Are you ready to pivot?

To move from the internal reality of our identity in Christ to the external demands of our daily lives, we must identify the specific callings God has placed on our calendars. By clarifying these various roles and responsibilities, we can ensure that our primary devotion to Christ rightly orders every other task we undertake.

Roles and Responsibilities

Have you ever heard someone say, "I don't need you to be my pastor right now. I just need a ________"? One of the greatest privileges of pastoral ministry is the way pastors become all things to all people, just as the apostle Paul exhorted the Corinthians (1 Corinthians 9:22). What an example of readiness to pivot in time to fulfill the need of the moment.

Pause here and complete a helpful exercise. Compose a list of all the roles in your life. Identify which contexts are the most effective for each. Your personal list might look similar to this:

Family roles

- Husband
- Father
- Son/Family Member
- Head of Household
- Primary Provider

Church roles

- Pastor
- Preacher
- Small Group Leader
- Biblical Counselor
- Vision-caster

Society roles

- Friend
- Neighbor
- Police Chaplain
- Community Leader
- City Volunteer

Who knew you were called to do so many wonderful things? Pastoral ministry surely becomes an incredible privilege when seen through the lens of your roles in the world. And beyond these various roles you also belong to what Martin Luther called "the common order of Christian love." This umbrella category describes the ordinary, God-given structures through which you express your gifting as a pastor and member of Christ's body. Luther wrote, "The Christian's worship is to serve the neighbor through love in the common order of daily life. God does not need your good works, but your neighbor does."[4] What additional ways do you use your gifts, perhaps as a writer, speaker, or supervisor in the wider world of God's work?

After you make your list, answer two questions: "Which of these areas are the most unfamiliar to you?" and "What area proves the most challenging for you?" Recognize the multiple time-dimensions you occupy. Roles in the home: father, husband, son. And you even have roles to play in other less obvious spaces: soccer field, small group, and the grocery store. You inhabit these roles across different settings, each with unique opportunities for ministry. This reality can feel overwhelming. How can we keep up so many roles with readiness?

Actually, mindful presence is not as complicated as it sounds. As you review your main roles, you will find ways in which they track along two or three roads. Let's call these the *roads of responsibility*. This important step in shepherding time will yield a number of helpful results. By identifying the few roads God has equipped you to travel, you will avoid mission creep—the tendency for church leaders to reach into the fringes and take on responsibilities best fulfilled by someone else. How many times have you lost control of time because you lost touch with your core roles in life and ministry? This age-old problem can be solved by identifying your main roads of responsibilities and sticking to them.

With every role comes responsibility, the requirements of a dutiful response. These could include actions, directions, or areas of oversight. Have you noticed a key theme running through this book? Effective pastors show an ability to know the need of the moment, and this truth shines brightest in the context of recognizing responsibilities.[5]

A difference exists between responsibility and concern. Concerns are the areas you would want influence and control over, but you do not have the scope of ability or context to exert influence. You simply don't have the power to give oversight in that area, most commonly because it falls under the responsibility of someone else. Thus, as you consider your key roles and roads of responsibility, you must recognize the limits of your ability and your particular calling.

> Recognize the multiple time-dimensions you occupy.
>
> ~ ~ ~
>
> *How do you currently recognize and respond to the different roles you inhabit throughout your day?*

You have much to gain and much to lose in this question of role and responsibility. Mature leaders know the difference between meager opportunities and meaningful ministry. A minister who is everywhere is nowhere. The pastor who takes on too much will perform nothing as he ought. In his book *The Reformed Pastor*, Richard Baxter writes with striking relevance, "Is it not more reasonable that you should pinch your flesh and family, then undertake a work that you cannot perform, and neglect the souls of so many of your flock?"[6] Because God has gifted you in many ways, you will always have more opportunities available to you than you can possibly handle. What a great problem to have!

But be alert. It does pose a problem. The longer you spend in faithful ministry, the more people will seek you out for help and service. It may sound cliché, but every pastor who shepherds time wisely will be a "no" man. He knows when to say no and has the wisdom and discipline to give his time to the most important roles and responsibilities.

Learning to say no to good opportunities is only possible when we understand the specific weight of the people God has placed directly in our path. This requires us to move beyond a general list of duties and into the intentional management of our primary relationships and the responses they require.

Relationships and Responses

Thinking through the many dimensions of pastoral ministry and the fleeting nature of time can feel like solving a riddle wrapped in a mystery inside an enigma. You can ready yourself with a clear sense of roles and responsibilities, and yet more thinking remains to be done. Again, pastors serve as ministers not mere administrators. A conversation about sorting roles and responsibilities might satisfy those who administer their work. But those who shepherd know a deeper dimension—relationships.

Our triune God exists in perfect relational unity with himself. His relational nature shapes how we inhabit time as pastors, and more broadly as Christians. In relationship to him, every person lives and moves and has being (Acts 17:28). Thus, shepherding always occurs in a relational space and not in abstract time. Caring pastors are aware of how they relate to others in the exercise of their roles and responsibilities. They care about how others experience their presence, tone, posture, and attentiveness. These aspects of personal ministry shape the time and effectiveness of every shepherd.

Shepherding people is a transformational act, not simply a transactional act. This engagement over time allows you to learn more about your relationship with others, both individually and in a room. You've heard about emotional intelligence, and here it is. The idea speaks to your ability to relate to others in time, and to match your response to the need of the moment.

Some people want solutions, some want understanding, and some simply want a non-anxious presence. In pastoral ministry, listening for the need of the moment can change everything. We can honestly admit together that not all pastors have a natural sense of what people need. God's grace helps us see clearly how we should spend the time we have with people.

> Learning to say no to good opportunities is only possible when we understand the specific weight of the people God has placed directly in our path.
>
> ~ ~ ~
>
> *Who are the specific people God has placed in your path to minister to in this season? How can you keep them in mind when considering other opportunities?*

If you assume a person wants advice when they actually long to be heard, you miss the important moment of ministry. But when you listen for the deeper need—help, hearing, or holding—you can shepherd people in ways that honor Christ, who entered our world, understood our need, and gave himself for us. Yet a common missing ingredient within such relational wisdom is the ability to make the pastoral pivot in time to meet the need of the moment. The danger of responding poorly usually relates to the fact that, although you know which realm you are functioning in, those around you don't. Are you interacting with someone as his or her pastor, church member, boss, or friend? This takes effort to make sure the person is aware of how you intend to use your time in that moment.

How nice it would be to have a simple formula by which we could navigate the many kinds of time we inhabit as pastors. Therefore, a goal and challenge of shepherding time must be to invest our time in such a way that we clearly recognize the role, responsibility, and relationship that fits the occasion so that we might give and receive grace as God works.

Mastering the pastoral pivot is not about a cold mastery of your schedule but a heart-level readiness to move between the various roles and relationships God has placed in your care. While these shifts between administration and shepherding may feel like a digression, they are actually the moments where your theology of time meets the reality of people's needs. By clarifying your role and responding to the need of the moment, you ensure that your time is not just managed but truly shepherded for Christ's glory.

Now that we have explored how to pivot gracefully through the day, we must turn to the practical discipline of evaluation. In the next chapter, we will move from the mindset of a shepherd to the accounting of time, learning how to track and assess our days to ensure our actual investment matches our ultimate calling.

Reflection Questions

1. How do you currently recognize and respond to the different roles you inhabit throughout your day? Where might you be unintentionally neglecting the gospel purpose of your time?
2. In what ways does your ability—or inability—to pivot between family, church, and societal responsibilities impact both your effectiveness as a pastor and your personal spiritual health?
3. Who are the specific people God has placed in your path to minister to in this season? How can you keep them in mind when considering other opportunities?
4. Who are the trusted individuals in your life who can help you maintain awareness of your roles, responsibilities, and relational contexts, and how can you invite them into your time stewardship process?

Action Step

For the next seven days, identify your two or three primary roles for the day and the one responsibility that matters most in each category. At the end of each day, briefly note where you pivoted well and where you lost clarity.

Chapter 7
Accounting for Your Time

QUANTIFYING PASTORAL TIME is challenging. This is why countless arguments arise with well-meaning elder teams who consider a pastor's work within a forty-hour framework. Every moment of a pastor's life is invested in the vocation of gospel ministry. All time is not the same for the pastor, and not all time needs the same level of care. To shepherd time is to guide time into moments that can be the most effective for gospel ministry. This is a definite shift from the marketplace mindset that doing more is better, but the treadmill of efficiencies does not make a helpful framework to consider time as a pastor. So, in this chapter, let's consider how to shepherd the different kinds of time that can morph daily and weekly.

Many pastors continue to view ministry hours the same way businesspeople view work hours. But they are simply not the same. We do not mean to suggest pastors should not steward time or conjecture that pastoral time should not be accounted for. The reality is that pastoral ministry is a lifestyle as much as a vocation.

The craft is not how to calculate for time but how to leverage time. Think about that word for a minute—*leverage*. The word has roots in the term *lever*, which refers to "a simple machine used to amplify force."[1] What a brilliant insight!

When we think of leveraging time, we do this very thing—amplify the force of our time (Ecclesiastes 9:10). Notice, we do not say "amplify the volume of our time." Being a time shepherd is not about working more hours but making those key ministry hours and efforts more effective, more forceful, more valuable.

Although the day has the same number of hours, their quality varies. Pastoral ministry aims to match the best hours with the best investments. Consider how long it takes to prepare for a sermon, do a hospital visit, forecast an all-church event, reconsider the budget, or invest in leadership development. This consideration recognizes that each of these efforts requires different kinds of attention to steward resources well. It is a strange calculation to consider pastoral ministry as efforts and not outcomes. We all wish we could control or leverage outcomes, but in the end, the only thing we can craft is our investment, so we shepherd ministry effort with the attention it requires.

This flexibility within pastoral time also delivers some special joys which not everyone else can experience. Cheerful pastors relish the flexibility they have to choose where time will best be spent. This is the meaning of leveraging time.

The craft of pastoral ministry is the intentionality of making the best use of time fruitful to gospel ministry (Psalm 90:12). Recognizing that there are more opportunities than time helps the pastor prioritize time toward the most useful end. Leveraging time is one way to consider how to prioritize time toward that end. Remember, the work of leveraging time is the work itself, not the ends. There is a temptation that if you leverage your time, then you will gain all your desired ends. We all know that is not the case (Proverbs 19:21). The work is leveraging and letting the Lord work the ends.

Living in the Long Wait

Every pastor (and perhaps every person) faces a great challenge of shepherding time because the second coming of Christ seems yet far off. After more than two thousand years of church history, we've settled in for a long haul. But with that long haul can come reduced vigilance against the fleeting nature of time. This God-ordained waiting raises a question of immeasurable import: How shall we live in the waiting? Jesus's teaching in Matthew 25 provides us solid help in answering this question. Let's closely consider the parable of the talents.

At the end of the previous parable of the virgins, Jesus exhorts his followers to be alert because they don't know the day or hour when he will return (Matthew 25:13). It makes good sense, then, we should want to consider how we should live in the waiting, what our lives should look like, and how we can invest ourselves in God's kingdom until his blessed return.

You know, this concept of waiting is quite familiar to us. Call to mind your daily experiences of waiting, like that of the ten virgins (think bridesmaids) who were waiting on the bridegroom to come for his bride. As a helpful exercise, think about all the waiting you do in daily life: in the pickup line for kids at school, at the doctor's office, or waiting to finally reach the grocery register. Did you know that one study found that the average person spends nearly 800 minutes per week waiting for various things? That means that over an average lifespan, each of us could spend five years just waiting. It begs the important question: In all of those little moments of waiting, what do you do?

Well, we all know what we do. As soon as a moment of waiting begins, out comes my phone because I simply can't afford to be bored. I can't just stand in line and think about my life, or pray, or make conversation with the fellow human standing behind me. But if we want to take our time, our lives, and the investment in God's kingdom seriously, we should consider what we do in the waiting. Think about those little moments, those 800 minutes per week. The average person can read comfortably about 200 words per minute. We sometimes call that pace "pulpit speed," because it matches the typical speed of a Scripture read publicly. Neither of us were math majors, but even we know in the amount of time one spends waiting in lines, we could read through the Bible fifty-five times. What a clear daily reminder of just how important it is to shepherd time effectively. It speaks to the kind of intentional focus Jesus thrusts upon us in the parable of the talents.

The first truth that Jesus intends to give us through this parable is that like the master in the parable, our Master entrusts us with resources for his glory—resources he intends for us to invest until he returns from his journey. The talents, which we'll explore more closely in a moment, image the resources and responsibilities he has entrusted to each of his servants.

Notice the words in verse 14. After commanding his disciples to remain alert, Jesus says, "For it is just like a man about to go on a journey. He called his own servants and entrusted his possessions to them. To one he gave five talents, to another two talents, and to another one talent, depending on each one's ability. Then he went on a journey" (Matthew 25:14–15). To understand the central message, we must first know what a *talent* is.

In the English language, we often think about talents as those little things that each of us do well. Some people have a talent for crossword puzzles, or some have a talent for public speaking. That does ring true in the parable, and yet in the typical definition of talent, we underestimate the significance of what the Master has entrusted to us.

Jesus has entrusted to us more than mere abilities. He has entrusted to each of us a multifaceted inventory of spiritual resources. By his grace in the gospel, God has redesigned our fallen ways into incredible potential, intending to invest us in his kingdom until he returns. All the while, by his Spirit, he remains present and working in us. First, we want you to realize anew the marvelous deposit Christ placed in you, as a Christian and as a church leader.

To make this truth clearer, consider what Jesus clearly means when he speaks of entrusted talents. At the time of the Olivet Discourse, his hearers recognized the word *talent* as a measurable currency. A talent referred to a seventy-five-pound lump or brick of silver, an enormous value. At that time, a talent amounted to 6,000 denarii, equal to 6,000 days' wages.

Let's do a little more math. Imagine you earn $65,000 every year for twenty years (that's 6,000 days of wages). The total would amount to one talent. How much is that? $1.3 million! Jesus says the master called his own servants and entrusted his possessions to them. To one, he gave five talents; to one, he gave two talents; and to another, he gave one talent.

What does that mean? The second servant, who received two talents, received $2.6 million, while the one with five received $6.5 million. This realization alone has radically changed how we think about our lives in light of the parable. Even if you are like us—a couple one-talent guys—you have received an enormous amount of kingdom resources and responsibility.

Who does this? Who goes on a journey, let's assume for twenty years, and doles out $10 million? Well, we know things about this man, because we know who he images. He is sovereign, wise, good, and happy.

Only a master absolutely assured of control would do such an extravagant act.

The master has wisdom—he knows what he is doing. Jesus never casts the master-character as a fool. He infuses with heavenly wisdom the decision to invest extravagantly in his servants.

The master exercises his goodness by distributing his possessions to the servants. It is with sovereign wisdom and goodness that Christ has, upon converting you and bringing you to himself by faith, given you an enormous set of resources that he intends for you to use until he returns.

He is sovereign, he is wise, he is good. He is also happy. He gives away his possessions with joy—welcoming his servants into his own life, wealth, and mission—and entrusts them with an almost inconceivable blessing. Friends, pastors, countrymen, lend us your ears. This is your life!

This parable is about you, your life, and God's seriousness about it. How does that change your vision for life and ministry? If nothing else, it brings an obvious question: What are you doing with your life? How are you living and serving in the waiting?

The year 2000 not only brought Y2K and a continuation of fear around the robotic uprising of the late 1990s, but the millennial turn also brought conference Passion OneDay to Memphis, Tennessee. The conference included a variety of bands and speakers, one of which was a lesser-known pastor named John Piper who preached a sermon which shaped a generation. If unfamiliar, you should watch it on YouTube.[2]

John Piper began by praying God would give him a prophetic word which would ripple out to the ends of the earth and into eternity. God answered Piper's prayer. In a climactic moment, he pulled out a *Reader's Digest* article which featured an aging couple who took an early retirement. He says, "Bob and Penny took early retirement from their jobs in the Northeast five years ago when he was 59 and she was 51. Now they live in Punta Gorda, Florida, where they cruise on their 30-foot trawler, play softball, and collect seashells." He stopped in that moment, and it was a moment that turned a generation upside down. Because up until that moment, to the crowd, it sounded like a perfectly fine thing to do—the American dream. You work hard, amass some resources, retire, and then relax. You cruise. But the next words out of his mouth turned the crowd silent. He simply said, "That's a tragedy. That's a tragedy."

> He [God] is sovereign, he is wise, he is good. He is also happy. He gives away his possessions with joy—welcoming his servants into his own life, wealth, and mission—and entrusts them with an almost inconceivable blessing.
>
> ~ ~ ~
>
> *How does your view of God—his character, generosity, and joy—shape the way you invest the "talents" he has entrusted to you in pastoral ministry?*

Then he imagined the retired couple standing before Christ on Judgment Day, saying, "Lord, Lord, see my shell collection." He said to the crowd, "Don't buy that dream. . . . as the last chapter before you stand before the Creator of the universe to give an account of what you did. Here it is, Lord—my shell collection. And I've got a good swing and look at my boat." He then concluded, "Don't waste your life. Don't waste it. You only have one. Risk it all for the glory of Jesus Christ." Piper's challenge cuts to the heart of the matter—but conviction alone is not a plan. We still need to know what faithful, risk-taking stewardship looks like in the ordinary stretch of days between now and eternity.

What We Do in the Waiting

The parable of the talents raises the question: What are you doing while you wait on Christ? It must affect you in some way because our Master has gone on a journey, entrusted us with enormous resources (some more than others), and one day he will return. As we use this first truth to provide some application to our lives, we would share with you a couple of pro tips. As you look at this passage, you will find something easy to do, but you must avoid it. Don't allow yourself to wrangle in questioning why one servant received five talents and another received only one talent. *Why does that pastor excel in ways I do not?* Focusing on the difference between five talents, two, and one will make you miss the point entirely. It's just not about that. Focus instead on the important stewardship of your own time as it relates to your particular calling.

The second pro tip to offer here is this: Don't make the easy mistake of underestimating the value of a single talent. It sounds like, "Oh, I just have one talent, what can I do?" Remember, at a minimum, you have received eternal resources valued at over a million spiritual dollars, and they have been entrusted to you so that you, with God's help, might multiply them in a way that increases the glory of your Master and your own happiness when he returns. You must know this first: Your Master has entrusted you with resources for his glory, and those resources are significant.

That brings us to a second truth we must embrace in order for this parable to take root in our pastoral lives: Every pastor—because of what the Master has entrusted to us in his kingdom—has an unavoidable stewardship. Looking again to Jesus's teaching in Matthew 25, notice the motivation of the faithful servants to actively engage with what has been entrusted to them. He says in verses 15–16, "Immediately," noting their urgency, expectation, and diligence. The first two servants immediately went to work multiplying the master's possessions. And they made no small improvement. The two faithful servants, in fact, doubled the master's value. Think about what this means—the servant who had been given $6.5 million has the joy of delivering back to his master today's equivalent of $13 million. The servant with two talents (which is equivalent to $2.6 million) sees an increase to $5.2 million.

They likely accomplish this by trading goods and property, buying and reselling grain, olives, and oil. Today we call this entrepreneurialism. Perhaps you need a shift of pastoral mindset which recognizes that every pastor is to act spiritually entrepreneurial.

The word *entrepreneurial* means to "undertake" an endeavor. It means to take action, pour out your energies, and invest all you have in the greatest endeavor possible—kingdom ministry. Again, if we fail to rightly estimate what Christ has given us, we will certainly not care much about shepherding time or living with purpose in the waiting.

But here comes a plot twist. The parable depicts a third servant who stands apart from the others. We read what the servant with one talent did. He went off the grid, into the country. He dug a hole in the ground and hid his master's money, and then after a long time, "the master of those servants came and settled accounts with them" (Matthew 25:18–19).

All three were entrusted with a stewardship, but only two were faithful stewards. It reminds us that there are two ways to exercise your calling: You will either invest your life into the world or into the kingdom. This kingdom stewardship comes from a comprehensive calling that does not end when we leave the church building. To avoid an off-the-grid passivity, we must bring a focused intentionality into the most private corners of our lives: our homes and our rest.

The Pastor at Home and Leisure

Certainly, our homes should provide a reprieve and rest from the challenges of ministry life. As we've considered, the pastoral life spans every moment of the day, both at the church building and in our own homes. The self-discipline considered above will open the door for increased joy and growth in our own homes as we shepherd our closest neighbors, those in our home.

The home will not shepherd itself, and every home and season is different. Consider the creative ways you can explore and enjoy your home. This is a place where you can experience the grace of God more freely than you can in your vocational ministry efforts. The demand is different, and the expectations are unique in the home compared to during the work week. Leverage your family relationships to experience the freedom of your love for Christ within a family who loves you. I promise there will be a benefit to the ministry you serve, but even if not, this effort of shepherding time and home is worth every moment.

> The first two servants immediately went to work multiplying the master's possessions.
>
> ~ ~ ~
>
> *Where do you see yourself investing your time like the faithful servants?*

The pastor at home

You may have heard it said that a pastor's time at home should not be seen as "off the clock" but rather a second shift. While the pastor's home provides a needed reprieve and rest, that does not equate to disengagement and solitude but a continued work of authentic pastoral ministry. Shepherding this time is to recognize the unique place that your family has in your life. They can tell very quickly if you're using your "pastor voice" or if you are being a godly member of the family.

The time at home is where shepherding is not restricted by programs and times but is in the ordinary. It is key for us to see time at home as a sanctified opportunity to live out what we believe without a public audience. This is the place where what you say you believe is recognized by those who live with you every day. There is a continuity of ministry effort as we always seek to promote biblical living and exalt the transforming work of the gospel. To see your time at home as an essential place of authentic ministry and not an escape from it, you will experience your home as a place of exploration and adventure.

The pastor at leisure

Leisure? you may think. *What leisure!? I'd love to have some, but my ministry life consumes almost all my time.* Still others among us have no problem finding leisure. Maybe your ministry life delights you in such a way that you feel it's all leisure. Good for you!

Regardless, every pastor needs to consider the role of leisure time in ministry. Certainly, a pastor can use too much pastoral leisure, but that's quite rare. Most pastors don't need help curbing leisure—they need help making time for it.

Every pastor needs time for intentional refreshment. The word *recreation* captures the best idea. The word helps us understand activities that promote flourishing or re-creating. This is especially vital for the pastor, because only having one week a year for vacation is not enough to truly refresh the mind and body. The pastor should consider and commit to regular activities that are for the purpose of personal refreshment. These are not activities that are to be considered discretionary but activities that are related to the personality and season of life that gives time away from the kinds of work and thinking that are demanded by ministry. Recreation gives respite from the daily demands yet enriches the person. This could be exploring a new craft or sport, or it could be organizing and beautifying your home. The expressions are only guided by productive rest. You will find some of your best insights and ministry efforts are inspired when you are in a state of recreation. It is worth it!

Some pastors have thought so little about the role of recreation that they don't even know where to start. Do you need to pick up a healthy and helpful recreation? Here are some ideas.

Choose a classic book or series. Begin slowly reading through it each day or a little each weekend. Twenty-five minutes a day or an hour on Saturdays will go a long way to developing a good leisurely reprieve.

Begin walking or running. Start slowly, and you'll find it one of the best additions to your life. It's a good time to listen to a podcast that interests you or just exercise in silence to sort out the details of life.

Or play some pickleball with a neighbor, join a bowling league, or find a weekend chess partner. You might be thinking, *Pickleball? Chess? Reading fiction? How boring!* So, find your own thing, whatever it is. But . . . find . . . your . . . recreation. You need it.

Shepherds of the Chief Shepherd

A final truth from the parable proves hard to handle. While faithfulness leads to reward, unfaithfulness leads to loss. As a result of their faithfulness, the first two servants are said to enter into their master's joy. We read in Matthew 25:20–23:

> The man who had received five talents approached, presented five more talents, and said, "Master, you gave me five talents. See, I've earned five more talents." His master said to him, "Well done, good and faithful servant. You were faithful over a few things; I will put you in charge of many things. Share your master's joy." The man with two talents also approached. He said, "Master, you gave me two talents. See, I've

> earned two more talents." His master said to him, "Well done, good and faithful servant! You were faithful over a few things; I will put you in charge of many things."

The same result: "Share your master's joy."

Then think of the third servant. Something has gone wrong. In verses 24 and 25, we read this about him: "The man who had received one talent also approached and said, 'Master, I know you. You're a harsh man, reaping where you haven't sown and gathering where you haven't scattered seed. So I was afraid and went off and hid your talent in the ground. See, you have what is yours.'" He went out, dug it up, and brought it back to him. Something tragic happens for a reason.

What do you notice about how this servant speaks to the master? It's a fascinating account, with details and dynamics which help us in our shepherding of time. Just as that servant made excuses and threw darts at the master's character, the master answers in verses 26–27: "You evil, lazy servant! If you knew I reap where I haven't sown and gather where I haven't scattered, then you should have deposited my money with the bankers, and I would have received my money back with interest." As we know, the unfaithful servant suffers a great loss.

This is the reality: If, in fact, that servant had been afraid, feeling overwhelming weakness and fear about what he would do with the resources given to him, and if he had deposited the money in the bank so that it would gain minimal interest—even just taking that step—the Master would have been understanding, merciful, and gracious.

But why does this happen to the third servant? Why has he not responded faithfully like the other two? Does he know the master? Are any of these things true about the master? Is he, in fact, a harsh man? Is he hard? Is he a taker? No. What's the problem? The unfaithful servant did not invest the master's resources because he was not operating in a true knowledge of the master's character and goodness.

Why were the faithful servants so generous in their investment? Why do they immediately and joyfully go out to multiply the master's fortune? Because they know him. They know what he is like. They know he is not harsh; he is gentle. They know he is not unjust; he is generous. It is because they know him that they shepherd the resources entrusted to them.

This speaks to the important dynamic of knowing the Chief Shepherd who has called you to serve as a shepherd under him. Therefore, the more you know him, the more you will give your life away. We've had this experience. You've probably had this experience, in earthly ways. We've known a number of mentors for whom we've poured out our lives. Why? Because we knew them. We wanted to please them, not out of fear, but because we admired their character. They weren't harsh to us, but merciful; they weren't unjust to us, they were generous. All that they invested in us gave us every motivation to pour our lives out for them.

Here's the point: If you have a wrong view of your Chief Shepherd, you will have a wrong use of your time; you will waste your ministry life. But if you have a right view of God, you will pour your life out in courageous stewardship. You'll take all kinds of risks and do it with a smile on your face because you know the Shepherd who has called you.

A final attempt to drive home the point comes from Puritan Walter Marshall and his book *The Gospel Mystery of Sanctification*. He writes, "You cannot love God if you are under the continual secret suspicion that he is really your enemy."[3] This provides a striking picture of the third servant who was under the constant secret suspicion that he believes his Master is his enemy. Marshall says, "We must be first persuaded of the love of God in Christ to us, before we can love God again with a holy love."[4]

Therefore, the ultimate key to shepherding time comes down to knowing God. Because you know him, he has given you incredible resources for his kingdom, for his glory. He is coming again, and all the while, he is working to develop them in you and activate your ability to be useful to him.

Clock Accountability

To succeed at shepherding time, you need some basic but helpful ways to account for your time. Until you're aware of how your time moves, you'll struggle to steward your time well.

One pastor sets a timer on his watch. Right now, it says 10 hours, 46 minutes, and 50 seconds, counting down until his ten o'clock bedtime. That timer descends before his eyes all day long, marking out the time he has left to use each day. He sets another timer for focused attention on the task at hand. Twenty-five minutes of focus, with a five-minute break. To some of you, that sounds burdensome. For this pastor, it is the delight of his life. It is his comfort, his joy. He loves nothing more than resetting the timer and then investing himself in what the Lord has entrusted to him. The benefit of such intentionality comes in the helpful way time remains in view and provides accountability to use it well.

Because the nature of pastoral time does not accord with the nature of business time, pastors need a different way to account for their investment of time in ministry. How should pastors track the time they spend on ministry life? Is tracking pastoral time even possible? We think it is possible, and we'll suggest another way to do it.

First, we don't recommend pastors track hours every week. That practice itself takes time and bears little regular benefit (unless a congregation or ministry supervisor requires it). Instead, we suggest tracking time periodically, by logging all hours in a week with notes on how you used your time. The periodic approach allows us to monitor ministry time investment without creating an overbearing system of time-logging every week. A myriad of helpful smartphone apps provide a user-friendly and free way to take inventory of your time and where it goes. Most of these tools allow you to create color-coded categories of time, and either clock in and out of them as you go or plug in the time spent in each area at the end of the day. Our experience shows an end-of-day time review approach provides the most friction-free option.

Furthermore, many of the applications will produce a report of how much time was spent in each category. It provides a way to visualize your investment in each activity. Here is an example:

1. **Sermon Preparation—27.5 hours**
   Time spent studying Scripture, writing, and revising sermons; often the single largest block of the week.
2. **Worship Services & Planning—5 hours**
   Leading services, coordinating music and liturgy, and reviewing service elements.
3. **Pastoral Care & Counseling—6 hours**
   Visiting the sick, counseling individuals or couples, responding to crises.
4. **Administration & Meetings—5 hours**
   Emails, phone calls, budgeting, supervising staff/volunteers, board meetings.
5. **Leadership & Vision Casting—3 hours**
   Long-range planning, mentoring leaders, ministry development.

6. **Community Outreach & Evangelism—3 hours**
   Meeting with community members, local events, outreach initiatives.
7. **Discipleship & Teaching—4 hours**
   Small groups, Bible studies, classes, or mentoring.
8. **Sabbath Rest & Personal Spiritual Growth—2 hours**
   Prayer, personal Bible reading, continuing education, retreats.

What a helpful tool! You can now see in context where your time has gone in the course of the week. You might consider meticulously tracking a week of time, perhaps, once per quarter. Then, compare each report to identify trends or adjustments needed. Should you transfer more time into sermon preparation? Does your own personal spiritual growth time need a boost? Has community outreach fallen off your weekly schedule? All of these questions find answers in a simple inventory of time.

Second, you need a guiding principle for tracking ministry time (Ephesians 5:15–16). We've already considered the challenge we face in recognizing when we are in ministry mode, and it poses a challenge for tracking time accurately.

A wise pastor we know suggests counting any time spent on any activity exclusively connected to his pastoral life. He asks, "If I were not a pastor, would I spend this time or do this thing?" If the answer is yes, then he doesn't include that portion of time in his inventory.

Again, we've noted the challenge. And while we both use this approach to monitor time, it does include a drawback. What about attending a baptism service when you have no responsibilities? Or what should you make of visiting an elderly saint in the hospital? Such common, ambiguous activities as these make the would-I-do-this-thing method a bit fuzzy.

Thus, a slightly different rubric may prove useful when taking periodic inventory of your pastoral time. Log the time which belongs to any of the following categories:

1. Time spent in intentional investment in the life of the church (e.g., vision-casting, sermon prep).
2. Time spent on activities required by the Bible, your congregation, or your ministry supervisor (e.g., staff meeting, hospital visits, managing attendance records).
3. Time spent in connection to your identity as a pastor (e.g., praying at city events, representing the church at local gatherings, discussing the church ministry with recent attenders).

While no perfect rubric exists, these three categories capture a broad swath of the time you spend as a pastor. Tracking the time periodically can help you keep a clear conscience about the faithful ministry you are performing, and it will help you know when you might be contributing an unhealthy amount of time, which can lead to family neglect or burnout.

Shepherding time focuses on effectiveness over the efficiency of doing more and more. The question is not, "What kinds of activities should I invest in to be a good pastor?" but rather, "How can I invest my time in ways that strengthen my pastoral role and lead to more effective ministry?" The art of shepherding time involves the exercise of sober thinking (Romans 12:3). We should consider how our lives may be spent with greatest effect and value. John Flavel reminds us that "the time of life is the time of opportunity."[5] No, pastors do not only do that which comes easy and naturally. At times church ministry feels like the easy work of breathing or riding a bike. Other times it feels like throwing a football with your weak hand. Truly, no smartphone app will replace wise accountability for your time. Yet taking inventory of your world (roles, responsibilities, personality, experience, desires, goals) must not be left behind. Instead, make a plan to take periodic inventory. Then ask trusted friends and your spouse about their observations. Together, these steps will help you think accurately about your time, in light of every life season, so you may invest your time wisely (Proverbs 15:22).

Reflection Questions

1. How does your view of God—his character, generosity, and joy—shape the way you invest the "talents" he has entrusted to you in pastoral ministry?
2. In what ways have you allowed a marketplace mindset (efficiency, output, professionalization) to distort your understanding of pastoral time and faithfulness?
3. Where do you see yourself investing your time like the faithful servants, and where do you see tendencies that resemble the third servant's fear, passivity, or suspicion toward the master?
4. What specific areas of ministry require your best "kind" of time, and how can you deliberately align your strongest hours with the most spiritually weighty responsibilities?
5. As you wait for Christ's return, what patterns of time-use reveal that you are leveraging the moments entrusted to you—and what patterns reveal drift, distraction, or neglect?

Action Step

Establish a morning and evening routine to frame your day. Write down what you'd like to include in both routines and aim to stick to them for a week. Journal the effects of these routines on your productivity and peace of mind.

Chapter 8
Planning the Ideal Week

WHO DOESN'T LOVE the idea of a perfectly planned week—but oh, how elusive it remains for many of us. Even though unforeseen events may interfere, having a plan still provides a helpful shape and structure to your rhythms of life and can highlight your priorities. In this chapter, we will lay out practical insights for planning the ideal week. These strategies will guide your own implementation of the stewardship principles we've discussed.

Productivity guru Michael Hyatt speaks of the ideal week as a tool for direction, not perfection. He says, "You have a choice in life. You can either live on purpose, according to a plan you've set. Or you can live by accident, reacting to the demands of others. The first approach is proactive; the second reactive."[1]

In one sense, this entire book has been focused on imperfections. We live in a broken world, as broken people fraught with distraction and disruption, in need of structure and focus. While we will never achieve the perfect week, each of us certainly can establish what we think of as the ideal week.

The ideal week is like laundry day. It doesn't happen on its own. You must schedule the sock reunion, or it will never happen. How much more does this apply to the plan for your entire week?

We've consulted with countless pastors who feel an incredible weakness around keeping it all together. Everything we've discussed in the previous chapters piles up on the average pastor, making it difficult to see through the clutter and into a better day. So let's do all we can to help solve this problem, with a highly practical chapter on planning the ideal week. We will provide three big things: a rationale, a structure, and tools to make it happen.

Within each of these, you will want to do three things. First, you need to establish clear priorities which align with your ministry values. These values will change depending on your station in ministry, capacity, and the specific calling which you have received. Second, once you can clearly state the main objectives your time will help you reach, you need to employ a system to ensure the important parts of the day will match the important tasks or purposes you control. And finally, to make this work, you need helpful and wise resources. Even the most knowledgeable and experienced carpenter cannot complete a project chopping, measuring, and fitting the wood with his bare hands. He has carpenter's tools to make his work precise and manageable. Thankfully, we live in the most resourced era of human history. We can put those resources to good use.

A Rationale for the Ideal Week

Establishing a weekly rhythm remains one of the keys to shepherding time. Do you like to dance? Those with rhythm dance with grace. Those who lack rhythm . . . well, let's just say it isn't pretty to look at. The same holds for your weekly routine of shepherding time. If you establish a good rhythm, your ministry will move with a bit more grace. If you lack rhythm, it won't be pretty. Remember, a low-friction rhythm will lead to highly effective ministry.

The rationale of shepherding time runs along the path of three concepts. Remember these concepts, and you will gain a healthy foundation for planning the ideal week. We should give careful attention to our weekly rhythm for three reasons.

First, time belongs to God, not us. Here lies a simple fact of reality. As we've considered together, Scripture does not treat time as a neutral commodity. Time is a precious thing, and we are very foolish if we let it slip away without improvement. We steward our time as creatures, living and serving under the Creator who is sovereign, wise, good, and happy. That means we do not live as autonomous managers of our own schedules, but servants who steward time under a good Master.

Second, the heart shapes our use of time. Certainly, shepherding time involves cold logistics of deciding what happens when. But in a far greater sense, shepherding time involves a deeper question of worship. We know the biggest challenges to healthy time management come from our hearts, not from the circumstances around us. Thus, our rationale for shepherding time remains deeply heart-oriented. Our time will always follow the direction of our heart's greatest loves. If we chase lesser things, no time management app can rescue us. Therefore, shepherding time means shepherding the inner pastoral life.

Third, and finally, calling clarifies the priorities of our weeks. We use the phrase "ideal week" to signify a stewardship of time which sets boundaries, establishes priorities, and frees us from the tyranny of the urgent so that we might fulfill the supernatural calling God has granted us. As we move forward, remember that priorities flow from calling, not pressure, guilt, or the expectations of others.

Therefore, maintaining a clear rationale for shepherding time will yield at least three benefits:

1. It will allow us to clarify priorities and allocate tasks in time which match our values.
2. It will reduce the common struggle we have with reactive decision-making, which only leads to an overwhelmed state of anxiety and trouble.
3. It will provide a framework by which we can review, reallocate, and improve our shepherding of time.

So with a healthy rationale in mind, let's turn next to the practical role of time blocking.

Pre-visualize Your Ideal Week

In order to plan the ideal week, we must begin with the big picture view of the week. You'll notice our approach moves from the macro to the micro, the wide-angle lens to the narrow angle. Drawing on our previous discussions about honing ministry priorities, we now take the next step of forecasting how the ideal week might unfold.

Consider this as the helpful practice of pre-visualizing. Don't fall for the temptation to skip ahead to the time blocking section of this chapter because you think it's the key that unlocks your weekly plan. Time blocking does provide a strong central structure to the ideal week. But forecasting the big picture serves a necessary step to prepare the pastor to fill those blocks of time with effective ministry.

In preparation for filming *The Phantom Menace*, George Lucas perfected the concept of pre-visualization, creating hypothetical storyboards of how the various scenes could unfold.[2] Now, every filmmaker does this to identify opportunities and challenges before setting the stage for filming. A similar tactic will help us as pastors to forecast how the ideal week might unfold. We're talking about a uniquely proactive and important consideration that enables us to manage time effectively.

As the first step in planning your ideal week, survey the various contexts of time which make up your regular ministry activity. Pre-visualize how those ministry tasks might naturally fill your week. To do this, make a list of all the kinds of ministry activities you do in a given week. Most of your list will contain the obvious weekly responsibilities like personal devotional time, sermon preparation, counseling appointments, administrative tasks, staff meetings, hospital visitation, local community engagement, study and growth, mentorship, and the like. Be sure to include activities you might often think of as non-ministry, like family time and personal exercise routines. If you need help completing this step, look back at the discussion of time pivots in chapter 6.

> Hold to the principle that the most important and time-consuming priorities will begin early in the week. And the lesser priorities will happen throughout the week or near the end.
>
> ~ ~ ~
>
> *Which priorities in your calling consistently get overshadowed by urgency or distraction?*

After you have compiled a list of all the activities you should accomplish in each week, begin to sketch out the best days and times for each of these activities. Think in chunks of time, not specific hourly appointment times. We will reach the point of laying out a specific time blocking schedule, but not yet.

You may find it helpful to compile your priorities and responsibilities into overarching themes and then tag each theme with a phase of the week: early week, midweek, or late week. For instance, your best sermon preparation likely happens early in the week. Yes, we know that Spurgeon prepared his sermons on Saturday night. But you're not Spurgeon, and neither are we. So hold to the principle that the most important and time-consuming priorities will begin early in the week. And the lesser priorities will happen throughout the week or near the end.

As you pre-visualize, consider the natural process of energy expenditure and rest. Most of us start the week with energy and motivation that wanes as the week passes. Account for this rhythm as you sketch out the ideal week. Place the more difficult themes and regular priorities early in the week, with the easier ones later. You may know this principle as "eating the frog." The frog represents your most challenging—and sometimes your least favorite—task or responsibility. You must choose when to eat it. Conventional wisdom suggests that you eat the frog first, because you can look forward with joy knowing the frog has been eaten.[3]

Let us show you a basic example of what pre-visualizing will produce.

Monday—Prayer, planning, and administration
Tuesday—Deep study and sermon preparation
Wednesday—Leadership and staff development
Thursday—Sermon finalization and care and counseling
Friday—Sabbath rest
Saturday—Family time, Sunday pastoral and personal preparation
Sunday—Worship, preaching, congregational ministry, and counseling care

Your pre-visualized week must become your own. What works best for you might not work best for another. But the main point of this exercise is to get a grip on the overall rhythm of the week. It allows you to enjoy a non-anxious anticipation of your best rhythm for life and ministry. Notice the previous example focuses on macro-items, not micro-items. If you jump ahead to sorting out all the miscellany of ministry and where it fits on your calendar, you will likely feel the crushing weight of overwhelm—and may end up bingeing Netflix with a bowl of ice cream, into which fall tears of grief and despair. Okay, maybe we're exaggerating. But you get the point. One step at a time.

The Bible reminds us that we are to consider and plan for things that are meaningful and important in life (Luke 14:28). The goal of tracking your time is not for a paycheck but for stewardship. Ask this question: "How can I best design an ideal week that will shepherd the time I have toward effective gospel ministry?" The focus of this question does not center ultimately around time on a clock but on our hearts and minds. It helps us determine how we might best engage with time, minimize distractions, and fulfill our callings effectively.

Why do you feel on some days like you accomplished little, even though you filled the day with many tasks and activities? We need to consider how creating a rhythm to the weekly calendar could help maintain a harmonious joy within all the events and activities which fill your days. Therefore, we turn attention to the slightly more specific task of time blocking.

Block Your Time

To say we have come merely to believe in the time blocking method understates the reality. We do not merely believe it. We live it, and it serves as the fundamental method of planning the ideal week.

Skilled time shepherds plan every day through a focused time blocking method, often in a structured journal or a Kanban-style organizational app.[4]

Whether you choose to handwrite your time blocking plan or use a fancy smartphone app, the point is this: Every pastor needs a way of accounting for or stewarding time, and the method of time blocking remains a tried-and-true method used by many efficient and effective pastors.

Time blocking (or time boxing) simply creates blocks of time in your weekly and daily calendar which are dedicated to specific priorities, projects, or tasks. A typical block of time ranges from one to three hours. Time blocking will allow you to further visualize your work, ensuring that nothing hides in mental clutter. It will also prevent you from taking on more tasks and projects than your time will actually allow. Establishing a time blocking structure to each day of the week provides the next step in our process of shepherding time. In one sense, you will have completed one step of time blocking when you complete the pre-visualizing step we shared above.

You should notice next that we suggest you follow a "multi-scale" time blocking, beginning with the pre-visualizing of your week and then moving to the step of marking out blocks of time dedicated to the most important tasks.[5]

Think for a moment about the term *multi-scale*. This means we should block time in the macro plan, the medium plan, and the micro plan of the ideal week. Pre-visualizing contains the big picture. General daily time blocking contains the medium plan, which we should consider next.

After the pre-visualization step, we move to assigning types of ministry work to blocks of time at a middle level of specificity. In the same way that you assigned big picture themes of ministry work to each day of the week, now you can assign more specific kinds of work to your daily schedule. Let us give you an example which you can work with to determine the best approach for you.

Think of your days in three large blocks of time:

Morning Block: 9 a.m. to 12 p.m.
Midday Block: 12 p.m. to 3 p.m.
Afternoon Block: 3 p.m. to 6 p.m.

You now can see your daily workflow in three phases. Because we enter each ministry workday fresh off a night of sleep, most of us do our best work in Phase 1. As we grow weary, our ability to focus deeply diminishes, and by the end of the day, we humble creatures need to recharge. Recognizing our creaturely rhythm and limitations suggests we plan our deepest work during Phase 1. This includes things like deep study of the Bible, sermon preparation, ministry writing, etc.

Then, to Phase 2 belongs somewhat less focus-heavy tasks, which you might call "knowledge work." These activities engage your heart and mind in a way that requires a kind of focus which is neither deep nor shallow, but somewhere between them. Phase 2 priorities include activities like one-on-one discipleship, counseling, staff meetings, etc.

Finally, Phase 3 contains the activities which require the least amount of focused attention. In keeping with the down ward progression, you might call this "shallow work." Do not hear the adjective *unimportant*. These tasks carry significant importance, but they do not require the same level of attention as *deep work* or *knowledge work*. We reserve the last portion of the ministry day for shallow work because our focused energies should be dropping off precipitously. Thus, tasks assigned to the shallow work block of each day include updating the church membership roster, tidying your workspace and email, etc. Let's add these details to our daily workflow phases:

Morning Block: 9 a.m. to 12 p.m.—Deep work
Midday Block: 12 p.m. to 3 p.m.—Knowledge work
Afternoon Block: 3 p.m. to 6 p.m.—Shallow work

But wait. One more thing. Add at the top and bottom the rest of the waking hours in your day. Let's assume you wake up at 7 a.m. and go to bed at 10 p.m. You should also block off the rest of your waking hours. We aim to account for every waking hour, which will allow us to make time not only for the ministry of our calling but also for the important personal and family time we all enjoy and need. And it will give us a place to plan various family activities like kids' activities, date nights, and more.

Personal and Ministry Mornings: 7 a.m. to 9 a.m.
Morning Block: 9 a.m. to 12 p.m.—Deep work
Midday Block: 12 p.m. to 3 p.m.—Knowledge work
Afternoon Block: 3 p.m. to 6 p.m.—Shallow work
Home and Ministry Nights: 6 p.m. to 10 p.m.

Congratulations! We just completed the second level of our multi-scale time blocking method.

Assign Your Tasks

Now you can complete the most energizing part of the process, true time blocking.

Continue a similar approach of evaluating your blocks of time and assign tasks to the blocks which fit best on the *micro-level*. This step is where the tangible victories are won, so let us tell you exactly what to do in three clear steps.

Step 1: Pray and review your mission and vision.
Step 2: List all your tasks for the week.
Step 3: Assign your tasks to suitable time blocks.

First, you must pray to seek God's help, focus, and wisdom. And with that help we can review the primary roles, responsibilities, and relationships which we considered in chapter 6.

Second, you may list every task needed for effective life and ministry in the coming days, and even weeks. This step may rightly be described as a *brain dump*. Choose your method—pen and paper, computer, smartphone. Scratch down every single item which comes to mind, and don't stop until you simply cannot think of anything else to add to the list. Include everything from sermon prep to calling your mom, from staff meeting to the after-school pick-up line. Everything. Leave nothing off this *brain dump* list.

However, before we conclude Step 2, we must add one more important detail. You should assign a projected amount of time to each task. Having a to-do list means little to our stewardship of time unless we prepare to spend the right amount of time. This simple step involves noting next to each task how much time it will take to complete. Thus, your list might look like this:

- Weekly staff meeting (2.5 hours)
- Counseling appointment with John Doe (1 hour)
- Prepare and print Sunday bulletins (1.5 hours)
- Schedule boiler repair (15 minutes)
- Visit the hospital (2 hours)
- Set agenda for church business meeting (1 hour)

And so forth . . .

Your list will appear much larger since it will include every task for the week. But with this small addition of projected task time, you can now take the last step.

Third, it's time to plan your ideal week. You know intrusive, unwanted distractions and disruptions will come. But you can proactively plan in such a way as to limit the destructive effects of these inner and outside forces. With your macro-level blocks in place (deep work, knowledge work, and shallow work), you should move each task into the appropriate block. Consider both time of day and day of week.

Start with the nonnegotiable items—those which must be done—before assigning the less urgent or important items. Once you have matched up all the items on your weekly list of tasks and projects, you will be able to identify any open periods of time. You're not finished until you've given every minute of the day a purpose. Remember, we want to shepherd all of our time to the glory of God. Be sure to block out intentional space for unexpected events. The blocking of buffer time fits within the strategy of giving every minute a purpose. Never underestimate the value of including purposeful margin in your schedule. A wise shepherd expects the unexpected—and keeps a few steps of margin for grace to walk in.

Do not merely find ways to busy yourself. This practice helps you account for all the time God gives by knowing where it all will go. It will empower you to account for your time, get your head around the many different actions you need to take, and avoid the common context-switching which plagues so many of us.

Before moving to a final chapter about the end of time, consider several tools which can help make your weekly planning work smoothly.

Tools for the Task

Do you realize we live in the most resourced era of human history? That's good news and bad news. Yes, social media, streaming services, smart devices, and artificial intelligence can cause a lot of trouble. But look on the bright side of all their benefits. We'll share a few of the most helpful tools as you seek to shepherd time in practical ways. We'll also provide a few bonus suggestions for more effective use of your time.

Analog tools for the task

Let's talk old school analog tools first. An older generation of pastors will love these. For yearly, monthly, weekly, and daily planning, the Full Focus Planner by professional leader Michael Hyatt works well. The name "Full Focus" accurately describes the planner's structure which accounts for your entire life: body, soul, family, work, and more. For those who want to plan thoroughly, resources like this can keep you focused and organized.

For those of you who prefer a slightly simpler and more immediate approach to time management, a basic time blocking worksheet may serve you well. You can find worksheet templates on our website, www.shepherdingtime.com.

If you find yourself benefiting from a highly visual and tactile approach to time management, you can build your own Kanban board with sticky notes. We explain how to do this at the website mentioned above.

Digital tools for the task

For the more modern tech-lovers, like Rush, a number of digital tools lay ahead in your journey toward better shepherding of time. The basic calendar app of your smart device or computer provides a good place to start. You can follow the steps for time blocking in a Google Calendar. Simply create a new calendar and call it "Time Blocking." Create blocks for the major portions of your day in a way that best matches your rhythm of joyful ministry throughout the week. These macro-level blocks of time will simply serve as visual markers of what kind of ministry could be planned throughout the day or week. Most calendars will even let you assign a color to your time blocks for easier visualization.

With those large blocks in place, you will assign tasks and projects within those blocked calendar segments. Thus, you can assign all your tasks to blocks of time and head into each new week with a clear plan laid out ahead of you.

With the advent of artificial intelligence, various automated calendaring options are developing before our very eyes. Only time will tell how well such tools will digitally help us with workflow planning.

Whatever you use, remember the goal of intentionality and stewardship reigns. A pastor can effectively pre-visualize, time block, and fulfill his calling, whether he's an analog or digital user. And whichever approach you take, do your best not to overcomplicate your life with too many tools. In this area, the saying holds: "Less is more."

Final Suggestions

Before we close this chapter and move on to the final one, we'd like to share a few final suggestions to help you in your noble quest to shepherd time.

Structure your day with prayer

It would surprise most people to hear that prayer often flies out the window when pastors become too busy. They might expect the opposite. But no. Like Martha, we pastors often lose sight of what matters most (Luke 10:38–42). Instead, we need to slow down, slow down, slow down—and spend time at the feet of the Master. One way to address this problem is through a daily routine of prayer. We've found it helpful to follow the daily prayers of John Calvin.[6] See them below and on our website, www.shepherdingtime.com. Allow these prayers to focus and guide you with dependence on God's grace and help.

Prayer upon Rising from Sleep

My God, Father, and Savior, since you have been pleased to give me the grace to come through the night to the present day, now grant that I may employ it entirely in your service, so that all my works may be to the glory of your name and the edification of my neighbors. As you have been pleased to make your sun shine upon the earth to give us bodily light, grant the light of your Spirit to illumine my understanding and my heart. And because it means nothing to begin well if one does not persevere, I ask that you would continue to increase your grace in me until you have led me into full communion with your Son, Jesus Christ our Lord, who is the true Sun of our souls, shining day and night, eternally and without end. Hear me, merciful Father, by our Lord Jesus Christ, Amen.

Prayer upon Beginning One's Work or Study

My good God, Father, and Savior, grant me aid by your Holy Spirit to now work fruitfully in my vocation, which is from you, all in order to love you and the people around me rather than for my own gain and glory. Give me wisdom, judgment and prudence, and freedom from my besetting sins. Bring me under the rule of true humility. Let me accept with patience whatever amount of fruitfulness or difficulty in my work that you give me this day. And in all I do, help me to rest always in my Lord Jesus Christ and in his grace alone for my salvation and life. Hear me, merciful Father, by our Lord Jesus Christ, Amen.

Prayer After the Midday Meal

O Lord God, I give you thanks for all the benefits and gifts you constantly shower on me. Thank you for sustaining my physical life through food and shelter; for giving me new life through the gospel; and for the certainty of the best and perfect life, which is yet to come. In light of all these blessings, I ask that you would not allow my affections to be tangled in inordinate desires for the things of this world, but let me always set my heart on things above, where Christ, who is my life, is seated at your right hand. Hear me, merciful Father, by our Lord Jesus Christ, Amen.

Prayer Before Sleep

O Lord God, now grant me the grace not only to rest my body this night, but to have my spiritual repose, in soul and conscience, in your grace and love, that I may let go of all earthly cares so I might be comforted and eased in all ways. And because no day passes that I do not sin in so many ways, please bury all my offenses in your mercy, that I might not lose your presence. Forgive me, merciful Father, for Christ's sake. And as I lay down in sleep to safely awake again only by your grace, keep me in a joyful, lively remembrance that whatever happens, I will someday know my final rising—the resurrection—because Jesus Christ lay down in death for me, and rose for my justification. In his name I pray, Amen.

Use the Pomodoro Method

Developed by Italian university student Francesco Cirillo in the late 1980s, the Pomodoro Method provides a basic plan for maximizing focus and effectiveness throughout the day. You only need a timer and a little discipline. Cirillo used a tomato-shaped kitchen timer to mark periods of focused work. The Italian word *pomodoro* means "tomato," hence the name.

To follow Cirillo's method, identify your next task and set a timer for twenty-five minutes. Give unbroken focus to the task at hand until the timer dings. Then set the timer for a short five-minute break. You earned it! These short breaks should contain idle time to allow your mind to rest. When this break timer dings, you've marked the completion of one "pomodoro." Reset the timer for twenty-five minutes of unbroken focus on the task at hand. Every four pomodoros, take a longer break of fifteen or twenty minutes. In the long run, the *focus on, idle off* format of the Pomodoro Method yields real results of effective productivity in your life and ministry. And a little-known secret—if you use the short breaks to accomplish mindless chores around the church or house, your staff or spouse will love you.

Establish a start-up and shut-down routine

Much of what we've considered in this book carries the value of structure for focused use of time relative to your calling. A daily start-up and shut-down routine can yield even better results for you. Following the typical spiritual discipline of Bible reading and intentional prayer (like the examples from John Calvin provided above) serves as a strong way to start your day. An early Godward focus sets the course of the day. But for many of us, the day's end brings the difficult challenge of stopping. You know this applies to you if your wife or friends tell you to learn how to put ministry aside for better life balance. You, especially, will benefit from a simple shut-down routine which marks the end of the day, and often a transition to family time. Cal Newport suggests employing a specific phrase or action to make the shutdown firm. He writes, "When you're done, have a set phrase you say that indicates completion." Newport uses the ritual phrase, "Shutdown complete." He continues, "This final step provides a simple cue to your mind that it's safe to release work-related thoughts for the rest of the day."[7]

In the next and final chapter, we need to conclude with a comforting reminder of exactly who shepherds our time, even when we struggle to keep up.

Reflection Questions

1. How does remembering that time belongs to Christ reshape the way you plan your week?
2. Which parts of your current rhythm reveal areas where your heart still resists his ownership?
3. Which priorities in your calling consistently get overshadowed by urgency or distraction, and how might pre-visualizing or time blocking help you steward those responsibilities with greater faithfulness?
4. As you consider your natural weekly energy curve, what specific changes could help you match your deepest work with your highest focus so that your ministry reflects both wisdom and dependence on the Lord?

Action Step

Experiment with the time blocking method for two weeks. Create a daily schedule that includes both work and leisure blocks, marking them clearly in your planner. At the end of two weeks, reflect on which parts of your schedule worked well and which didn't.

Chapter 9

The Ultimate End of Time

WELL, YOU'VE REACHED the end. We began this journey about shepherding time where we must—with God who is our eternal present. And we must bring this book to a close by returning to where we began.

This book has focused your attention on many important aspects of the pastor's time and his ability to utilize each moment for God's glory. Our view of time has been elevated to see it as a precious commodity which must be shepherded well. This work requires a number of practical steps like establishing priorities, creating actionable plans, and engaging in reflective practices. It leans into focused relationships and watches carefully for the thieves which steal away the precious moments we have for spiritual growth, personally and among the people we serve. But the art of shepherding time cannot be relegated to the mere practical.

We close now with a final encouragement to view all shepherding efforts in the light of eternity. You see, the ultimate concern of this book has not centered on merely watching the clock and staying busy. Instead, the heart of every page aims to embrace the transient in light of the eternal joy of knowing God ordains our day for his glory and the sinner's joy.

We must in the end reflect on the ultimate perspective of time management within a biblical framework, drawing from

Ecclesiastes 3:1–3 and 12:13–14. You know these words well, both from Scripture and as the words which inspired the lyrics to "Turn! Turn! Turn! (To Everything There Is A Season)" by the musical group The Byrds. "There is an occasion for everything, and a time for every activity under heaven: a time to give birth and a time to die; a time to plant and a time to uproot; a time to kill and a time to heal; a time to tear down and a time to build" (Ecclesiastes 3:1–3). There is a time for everything.

> View all shepherding efforts in the light of eternity.
>
> ~ ~ ~
>
> *What are some ways you can cultivate an eternal perspective in your daily time management?*

Throughout this book, we've argued that shepherds should be intentional about maximizing their time. Hopefully, you can see more clearly that this endeavor moves far beyond time management; it underscores the idea of caring for time as the context for gospel ministry, regardless of role, relationship, or circumstance. Mark this invaluable word from Jonathan Edwards: "Time is precious, and ought to be improved with the utmost care."[1] There certainly can be a sense of overwhelm as we strive to bring this level of intention to moments of life. And yet, we have before us the constant reminder that no matter what kind of time we inhabit, we do so under the loving providence of the God who holds all time together, and who gives us hope and courage in every moment and season. He does this through Christ, who came for us in the fullness of time. He enables us to live in every present, yet fallen moment, with hope.

Embracing the Ephemeral

The book of Ecclesiastes seems to signal a dark conclusion. After all, isn't the preacher of Ecclesiastes fixed on life as a "vanity of vanities"? While the author does speak of vanity, the central point does not convey meaninglessness but rather the fleeting nature of time—here one moment and gone the next.

In this sense, time is ephemeral; one moment passes into the next like a mist. What should this mean for us as pastors? Despair? Retreat? By no means. We instead should feel the joy and power of presence. To every moment belongs a mixture of good and evil, joy and sorrow. But through the good news of Christ, we know the assurance of God's favor and help in every hour.

There is joy in being present and resting in the sovereignty of God, who holds your past and future perfectly. The careful-minded pastor knows a deep sense of divine contentment, allowing him to enjoy the moments and ministry opportunities God has planned for him.

Investing in your life the principles of this book will focus on shooting today's arrows with tomorrow's targets in view. We aim and engage but ultimately do not know how God will use all of those moments to accomplish his desired ends. What we do know, however, is that he is sovereign, wise, good, and happy. Thus, investing our lives in God's promises for today, and knowing they will come to fruition, presents a daunting challenge. And yet, God's loving ordination of our days assures us we do not live in vain (Psalm 139:16).

The End of Time

The preacher of Ecclesiastes brings these pages to a close by stating the conclusion of the matter. He writes, "When all has been heard, the conclusion of the matter is this: fear God and keep his commands, because this is for all humanity" (Ecclesiastes 12:13). All of life finds its fulfillment in one great mission—to love God and follow his loving leadership in our lives. And that, dear friends, always remains the central goal within the art of shepherding your time.

Shepherding time is not about doing more, or being someone better than you are, or impressing those around you with all you can accomplish. Instead, shepherding time is about engaging in timely moments with a transcendent desire to love God, know the joy of keeping his commandments, and shepherding others to do the same (Psalm 119:14–24).

> There is a time for everything.
>
> ~ ~ ~
>
> *How does seeing time as seasonal help as you consider different ways to shepherd time?*

At the end of the book of Ecclesiastes, the preacher finds help and hope knowing that although our days are ephemeral and fleeting, there will come a day when everything will be made right and good forever. There is a day coming when all time will be perfectly shepherded by the Great Shepherd, Jesus Christ. Our efforts today will reach their completion when Christ makes all things new.

Therefore, you don't need to make time; you just need to make the most of the time you have. That may sound cliché, but it's true. Being intentional in the present is investing in what will last eternally—God, God's Word, and the souls of people everywhere.

God has ordained time to mark our lives in earthly humanity, with all its struggles and joys, knowing that we have not yet reached the end. By grace, we can pour out our time with hope that one day we will experience the whole of what we are today pursuing in part.

Reflection Questions

1. How does seeing time as seasonal help with the different ways to shepherd time?
2. What are some aspects of time that you have demanded to be more than it was intended to be?

3. How do the promises of God at the end of time shape how we pursue shepherding time?
4. What are some ways you can cultivate an eternal perspective in your daily time management?

Action Step

Create an "Eternal Perspective List" that outlines how the time you spend—or waste—impacts your spiritual life and your ministry. Reflect on whether you've been investing in eternal matters or temporal concerns and make a plan to adjust your priorities accordingly.

Appendix A:
Practicing Sabbath

THROUGHOUT THIS BOOK, we have focused on the practical tools and disciplines which help us to shepherd time with wisdom. However, a healthy stewardship of our hours stands incomplete if it neglects to maintain an eye on the regular rhythms of Sabbath rest. We have included this appendix because rest must not be seen as a diversion from our pastoral calling, but as a vital part of shepherding our time. We hope you will move beyond seeing time as a resource to be spent and begin to see it as a trust to be stewarded. A stewardship that must include the rhythms of rest from our work, as God designed rest for our good. As you read, we hope you take away a renewed conviction that your effectiveness in ministry is not fueled by constant activity, but by a heart that is consistently re-anchored in the rest of Christ. Sabbath transcends mere understanding; it demands embodiment. This rhythm offers a divine gift while requiring an important discipline. Though our culture prizes productivity and efficiency, Sabbath defies these norms for our good. This practice of Sabbath humbles us, proving we are neither machines nor self-sustaining creatures. As created beings, we flourish only through rest, renewal, and a conscious dependence on God.

Sabbath centers on trust. Stopping our work acknowledges that the world continues without us. We recognize God's activity even during our inactivity. This realization gives life to our ministry contexts, where endless work and unmet needs often overwhelm us. Sabbath interrupts the lie that everything depends on our effort. It reorients our hearts to remember God as the true Shepherd and ourselves as simple stewards.

Practicing Sabbath calls for a special intentionality; it never occurs by accident. Left alone, we fill every moment with work, ministry, and other activities—all good or meaningful tasks. But Sabbath calls us to something different: stop, rest, and delight. Answering the Sabbath call requires preparation. Just as we prepare for a feast or a critical meeting, we must prepare for the Sabbath.

Preparation blends practical and spiritual awareness. Practicality includes blocking time for rest, setting communication boundaries, and scheduling life-giving activities. Spiritually, we must cultivate an awareness of our limits. We must monitor our souls throughout the week, recognizing when we feel depleted or disconnected, and then respond by carving out space for rest.

Sabbath carries a communal dimension, as well, which we should not ignore. While individuals practice it, the rhythm bears more fruit when a community understands and supports it. This circle includes your family, ministry team, and church. As we've discussed throughout *Shepherding Time*, communicating your Sabbath rhythms sets expectations and fosters shared understanding. It also models healthy patterns for those under your care. In this way, your Sabbath practice provides both personal renewal and a unique, pastoral impact on others.

Sabbath rejects a one-size-fits-all mold. Its form varies according to seasons of life, personality, and context. Some might manage a full day of rest, while those in demanding seasons might begin with a few intentional hours. We find again what we know: Faithfulness matters more than rigidity. We must set apart time for renewal regardless of the duration. One wise mentor advised us as pastors to identify the minimum necessary Sabbath rest each week and start there, rather than aiming for an unreachable ideal. This proved helpful advice.

As a result, we will find the help we need to distinguish between mere cessation and true rest. Again, Sabbath involves more than the absence of work; it requires the presence of restoration. This restoration touches spiritual, physical, and interpersonal areas of our lives.

Spiritually, Sabbath incorporates prayer, Scripture, silence, and worship. Physically, it may include sleep, exercise, or joy-filled hobbies. Interpersonally, it means seeking people who refresh you.

Furthermore, to shepherd time we must distinguish Sabbath from ministry work. Activities that give life to others often feel like work to the leader. Sabbath invites you to shed the common professional mindset and engage in activities free from output or expectation.

Never let Sabbath become another burden or checklist. It does not require a perfect day or rigid rules. Instead, it cultivates a posture of restfulness and dependence. If Sabbath triggers guilt, we will miss its purpose. Seek presence with God, yourself, and others rather than perfection.

Another wise reminder calls us to drink before we are thirsty. This principle captures the essence of Sabbath. Waiting for total exhaustion proves both unwise and unsustainable. By that point, rest becomes mere recovery rather than true renewal. In this, we can see that Sabbath functions as a preventative rhythm, not a reactive last resort. Consistency fuels this rhythm. Just as sleep, diet, and exercise build long-term health, so does Sabbath. Sporadic rest cannot replace the benefits of a steady pattern. A weekly Sabbath builds a foundation for resilience, clarity, and spiritual vitality. It allows us to lead and serve from spiritual fullness rather than from a place of depletion and exhaustion.

Eventually, this practice of Sabbath shapes our identity rather than just our schedules. We see ourselves not as a worker but as one loved and sustained by God. Our sense of value shifts from what we produce to what it means to be in relationship with God. Indeed, this shift transforms our approach to ministry, relationships, and life.

Ultimately, Sabbath offers an invitation. It invites us to rest in God's presence, trust his provision, and experience his loving care. Do not resist or minimize this gift; embrace it as essential to faithful ministry and life.

Begin your Sabbath practice with small, intentional steps. Identify what truly restores you. Invite a trusted friend to discuss these goals. Set aside time, communicate your plans to those close to you, and prepare your own heart for refreshment. Over time, these small steps will form a rhythm that sustains you and reminds you of the grace that meets you in your resting, not your striving.

Appendix B: Recommended Resources for Further Reading

Richard Baxter, *A Christian Directory: Or, A Body of Practical Divinity and Cases of Conscience*. London: Robert White, 1673.

Tim Challies, *Do More Better: A Practical Guide to Productivity*. Cruciform Press, 2015.

Kevin DeYoung, *Crazy Busy: A (Mercifully) Short Book about a (Really) Big Problem*. Crossway, 2013.

Reagan Rose, *Redeeming Productivity: Getting More Done for the Glory of God*. Moody Publishers, 2022.

Dave Harvey, *Rescuing Ambition*. Crossway, 2010.

R. Kent Hughes and Barbara Hughes. *Liberating Ministry from the Success Syndrome*. Tyndale House, 1988.

Charles E. Hummel, *Tyranny of the Urgent*. InterVarsity Press, 1967.

Christopher Ashworth Lane, *Zeal without Burnout: Seven Keys to a Lifelong Ministry of Sustainable Sacrifice*. The Good Book Company, 2016.

Matt Perman, *What's Best Next: How the Gospel Transforms the Way You Get Things Done*. Zondervan, 2014.

Jordan Raynor, *Redeeming Your Time: 7 Biblical Principles for Being Purposeful, Present, and Wildly Productive*. WaterBrook, 2021.

James K. A. Smith, *How to Inhabit Time: Understanding the Past, Facing the Future, Living Faithfully Now*. Brazos Press, 2022.

For coaching, consulting, and other resources to help you shepherd your time, visit www.shepherdingtime.com.

Notes

Chapter One

1. *Becoming Warren Buffett*, directed by Peter W. Kunhardt (HBO Home Entertainment, 2017), DVD.

2. Thomas Watson, *The Godly Man's Picture* (Edinburgh: Banner of Truth Trust, 1992), 207.

3. Thomas Brooks, *Precious Remedies Against Satan's Devices* (1652; repr. Banner of Truth Trust, 2021), 112.

4. Geoffrey Chaucer, *The Canterbury Tales*, trans. Nevill Coghill (Penguin Books, 2003), 125.

5. Ted Chiang, *The Merchant and the Alchemist's Gate* (Subterranean Press, 2007), 71.

6. Thomas Adams, *The Works of Thomas Adams*, vol. 1 (James Nichol, 1861), 56.

7. Walter Henegar, "Putting Off Procrastination," *Journal of Biblical Counseling* 20, no. 1 (2001): 41.

8. Jonathan Edwards, *The Works of Jonathan Edwards*, vol. 1, ed. Sereno E. Dwight (Banner of Truth Trust, 1974), xx.

Chapter Two

1. *The Twilight Zone*, created by Rod Serling. Cayuga Productions and CBS Television Network, 1959–1964.

2. Richard Baxter, *The Reformed Pastor*, ed. Tim Cooper (Crossway, 2021), 67.

3. Timothy Keller, *Center Church: Doing Balanced, Gospel-Centered Ministry in Your City* (Zondervan, 2012), 275–78.

4. John Calvin, *Institutes of the Christian Religion* 4.1.1.

5. C. H. Spurgeon, "The Preaching of the Word," in *The Metropolitan Tabernacle Pulpit*, vol. 15 (London: Passmore & Alabaster, 1870), 517–28.

Chapter Three

1. D. A. Carson, "8 Lessons from the School of Prayer," *The Gospel Coalition*, 2023, www.thegospelcoalition.org/article/8-lessons-from-the-school-of-prayer/.

2. Frederick W. Danker, rev. and ed., *A Greek-English Lexicon of the New Testament and Other Early Christian Literature*, 3rd ed. (University of Chicago Press, 2000), 878. The term προσευχή (*proseuchē*) denotes prayer directed toward God, often with the nuance of ongoing communion and petition.

3. Charles H. Spurgeon, "Sermon 2437," in *Metropolitan Tabernacle Pulpit*, vol. 41 (1895), 518.

4. John Piper, *Brothers, We Are Not Professionals: A Plea to Pastors for Radical Ministry*, rev. and expanded ed. (B&H Publishing Group, 2013), 1.

5. Cal Newport, *Slow Productivity: The Lost Art of Accomplishment Without Burnout* (Portfolio, 2024), 20.

6. Richard Baxter, *The Reformed Pastor* (London: T. Parkhurst, 1656), 12.

7. John Wesley, *The Letters of the Rev. John Wesley, A. M.: 1758*. Wesley Works Editorial Project, 1758, "To Mrs. Wesley," January 27, 1758, Wesley Center for Applied Theology, NNU.

8. Tim Keller's focus on contextualization centered on both affirming and confronting culture—in the way of a "gentle shaping" of culture. See more on Keller's approach by visiting Redeemer City to City (https://redeemercitytocity.com/).

9. For more on gently shaping your church culture, see Mark Dever, "Preach, Pray, Love, and Stay," *9Marks*, 2005, www.9marks.org/article/preach-pray-love-and-stay/. Also see www.shepherdingtime.com for more resources on this topic.

Chapter Four

1. Charles M. Schulz, *Peanuts*, July 13, 1954.

2. Richard Baxter, *A Christian Directory* (1673; repr., Soli Deo Gloria, 1990), 1:308.

3. The phrase "with a high hand" appears in the footnote for Numbers 15:30. It's the literal translation of "who acts defiantly."

4. Chris Martin, "5 Social Media Stats Pastors Should Know," *Lifeway Research*, March 3, 2022, https://research.lifeway.com/2022/03/03/5-social-media-stats-pastors-should-know/.

5. Ed Welch, "Feeling Guilty? Who Doesn't?" *Christian Counseling & Educational Foundation (CCEF)*, April 14, 2016, www.ccef.org/resources/blog/feeling-guilty-who-doesnt/.

6. Martin Luther, *Luther's Works, Vol. 54: Table Talk*, ed. and trans. Theodore G. Tappert (Fortress Press, 1967), 447.

Chapter Five

1. Cotton Mather, *Essays To Do Good: Addressed To All Christians Whether in Public or Private Capacities* (The American Tract Society, 1838), 30.

2. "Science Quotes by Edward A. Murphy, Jr.," Today in Science History, accessed November 24, 2025. https://todayinsci.com/M/Murphy_Edward/MurphyEdward-Quotations.htm.

3. John Flavel, *The Mystery of Providence* (Thomas Parkhurst, 1678), 14.

4. S. M. Lockridge, "It's Friday, But Sunday's Coming," Sermon Audio, accessed November 24, 2025, https://media-cloud.sermonaudio.com/text/412171356329.pdf.

5. Charles H. Spurgeon, "Sermon 2829," in *The Metropolitan Tabernacle Pulpit*, vol. 49 (Pilgrim Publications, 2002), 271.

6. John Calvin, *Institutes of the Christian Religion*, vol. 1, ed. John T. McNeill, trans. Ford Lewis Battles (Westminster Press, 1960), 108.

7. Jerry Bridges, *Respectable Sins: Confronting the Sins We Tolerate* (NavPress, 2007), 10.

Chapter Six

1. Thomas Watson, *Heaven Taken by Storm; or, The Holy Violence a Christian Is to Put Forth in the Pursuit After Glory*, In the digital collection Early English Books Online. https://name.umdl.umich.edu/A65299.0001.001. University of Michigan Library Digital Collections. Accessed April 17, 2026.

2. Brother Lawrence, *The Practice of the Presence of God: Conversations and Letters of Brother Lawrence of the Resurrection*, trans. Robert J. Edmonson (Paraclete Press, 2010).

3. Brother Lawrence, *The Practice of the Presence of God*, trans. E. M. Blaiklock (Thomas Nelson, 1982), 25.

4. Martin Luther, *Treatise on Good Works*, in *Luther's Works*, vol. 44, ed. James Atkinson (Fortress Press, 1966), 23.

5. Paul David Tripp, *Instruments in the Redeemer's Hands: People in Need of Change Helping People in Need of Change* (P&R Publishing, 2002), 226–28.

6. Richard Baxter, *The Reformed Pastor* (London: T. Parkhurst, 1656), 97.

Chapter Seven

1. *Merriam-Webster Dictionary*, "Lever," accessed November 24, 2025, https://www.merriam-webster.com/dictionary/lever.

2. John Piper, "Boasting Only in The Cross—John Piper—Passion OneDay 2000," conference session, posted March 19, 2015 by Desiring God, YouTube, https://www.youtube.com/watch?v=XajXpH908Yg.

3. Walter Marshall, *The Gospel Mystery of Sanctification: Growing in Holiness by Living in Union with Christ*, reprint (Christian Focus, 2004), 236.

4. Marshall, *The Gospel Mystery of Sanctification*, 237.

5. John Flavel, *The Mystery of Providence* (1678; repr., Edinburgh: Banner of Truth Trust, 1963), 27.

Chapter Eight

1. Michael Hyatt, "How to Better Control Your Time by Designing Your Ideal Week," Full Focus, December 12, 2024, https://fullfocus.co/ideal-week/.

2. Lucas Seastrom, "Phantom at 25: Ben Burtt Talks Sound Design and Picture Editing with George Lucas," StarWars.com, May 22, 2024, https://www.starwars.com/news/ben-burtt-the-phantom-menace.

3. Brian Tracy, *Eat That Frog! 21 Great Ways to Stop Procrastinating and Get More Done in Less Time* (Berrett-Koehler, 2001).

4. Kanban is a workflow-management method in which each card contains a task or project and your work is visualized in a series of lists and cards. You can Google "Kanban" to see a number of apps to consider.

5. Tim Ferriss, "The Tim Ferriss Show Transcripts: Insights from Tara Brach, Ryan Holiday, Maria Popova, and Cal Newport (#626)," *Tim Ferriss* (blog), October 11, 2022, https://tim.blog/2022/10/11/insights-from-tara-brach-ryan-holiday-maria-popova-and-cal-newport-transcript/.

6. John Calvin, "Appendix: Forms of Prayer," in *The Catechism of the Church of Geneva*, trans. Elijah Waterman (1815; Project Gutenberg, 2010), www.gutenberg.org/ebooks/98723.

7. Cal Newport, *Deep Work: Rules for Focused Success in a Distracted World* (Grand Central Publishing, 2016), 151.

Chapter Nine

1. Jonathan Edwards, "The Preciousness of Time and the Importance of Redeeming It," in *The Works of Jonathan Edwards*, 2:233.